Scarecrow Professional Intelligence ~~~~~
Series Editor: Jan Goldman

WRITING CLASSIFIED AND UNCLASSIFIED PAPERS IN THE INTELLIGENCE COMMUNITY

James S. Major

Jan Goldman
Series Editor

*Scarecrow Professional Intelligence
Education Series, No. 4*

The Scarecrow Press, Inc.
Lanham, Maryland • New York • Plymouth, UK
2009

SCARECROW PRESS, INC.

Published in the United States of America
by Scarecrow Press, Inc.
A wholly owned subsidiary of
The Rowman & Littlefield Publishing Group, Inc.
4501 Forbes Boulevard, Suite 200, Lanham, Maryland 20706
www.scarecrowpress.com

Estover Road
Plymouth PL6 7PY
United Kingdom

British Library Cataloguing in Publication Information Available

Library of Congress Cataloging-in-Publication Data

Major, James S.
  Writing classified and unclassified papers in the intelligence community /
James S. Major.
      p. cm. — (Scarecrow professional intelligence education series ; No. 4)
  Includes bibliographical references and index.
  ISBN-13: 978-0-8108-6192-3 (pbk. : alk. paper)
  ISBN-10: 0-8108-6192-5 (pbk. : alk. paper)
  ISBN-13: 978-0-8108-6278-4 (ebook)
  ISBN-10: 0-8108-6278-6 (ebook)
  1. Open source intelligence–United States–Authorship. 2. Military
intelligence–United States–Authorship. 3. English language–Style. 4. English
language–Usage. I. Title.
  JK468.I6M3335 2009
  808'.066327–dc22   2008030697

∞™ The paper used in this publication meets the minimum requirements of
American National Standard for Information Sciences—Permanence of Paper
for Printed Library Materials, ANSI/NISO Z39.48-1992.
Manufactured in the United States of America.

Contents

Foreword

One of the most important considerations of being a professional is that every profession requires standards. Any profession, similar to any closed community, must have agreed-upon reference material to communicate and disseminate information to its members. Typically, this is done through established training, education, and years of experience.

Intelligence relies on transmitting information to those who will link it to additional information or immediately forward it to someone who will put that information into context or action. Only then does it become intelligence. Writing is the *raison d'être* of the intelligence professional. It is the primary basis of collecting, analyzing, and producing intelligence. Effective writing equips the intelligence professional with the communication and thinking skills needed to be successful.

It may come as a surprise, but there are few writing standards available for the intelligence professional. Without a doubt, writing is a personal outlet for the individual; but it should not be confused with the *style* one uses. *How* a person writes should never be confused with *what* a person writes. There must be form and standards within a profession, or it becomes merely a disparate group of individuals, not a profession.

In the intelligence community there is no standard style guide. There is the *U.S. Government Printing Office Style Guide,* used by some agencies and individuals inside and outside of the intelligence community. However, given the specific nature of writing intelligence products, including both classified and unclassified sources, that manual is inadequate for those demands.

Over time, several style guides have been used in the intelligence community. The three most popular include the *Modern Language Association Style Guide* (MLA), *the American Psychological Association Style Guide* (APA), and the *Chicago Manual of Style*. Depending on where a person went to school, it is likely he or she is using one of those style guides, if any style guide at all.

Meanwhile, some professions develop their own style guides that are not widely used except by its own members—for example, the style guides used by the American Anthropological Association and the American Medical Association. In journalism, the *Associated Press Style Guide* is used by most newspapers, while larger and more established publications such as the *New York Times* have their own style guides.

As the U.S. Government seeks to develop a more common national intelligence community environment, it is time to initiate and develop a common style guide that transcends organizational lines of communication. This book is unique because it includes how to handle classified information as well as unclassified information, which no other style guide includes. This book complements Jim Major's previous publication in the series, *Communicating Intelligence: Writing and Briefing in the Intelligence and National Security Communities*. Consequently, this book seeks to establish a standard for a profession that is especially dependent on rapid and effective communication.

Jan Goldman, Ed.D.
Series Editor

Introduction:
The Need for Standards

Imagine that you're remodeling a bathroom, and part of that project includes a new shower curtain. You go to your favorite store and buy a colorful shower curtain along with a liner and the rings to hold them up. When you get home and unwrap your new accessories, you notice that there are only eight rings, but the curtain has twelve holes and the liner has ten! What now?

If you've ever had an experience like that, you doubtless wondered who was in charge of the standards. I experienced a revelation years ago when I bought those items and noted that the shower curtain was made in China, the liner in the Philippines, and the rings in Korea. But despite the geographical disparity, the curtain had ten holes at the top; the liner's ten holes matched the curtain's perfectly; and there were ten rings. That experience made me appreciate the fact that someone had established standards for such things, and that I had benefited from it.

What, you may ask, does that anecdote have to do with a book about writing style and format? The point here is that every college, university, agency, and organization has—or certainly *should* have—established standards for how they do business, including specified forms and formats for writing. It might be called a style guide, standing operating procedures, or a continuity book—but it is there, and its intent is to ensure appropriate standards for the organization. In academia, standards for papers allow professors to focus on content without wasting time on issues of form and format; in the Intelligence Community, those standards are reflected in the products distributed to consumers, enabling a user to know immediately where to look for information.

In 1985 I joined the faculty of the Defense Intelligence College (now the National Defense Intelligence College) in Washington, DC. My assigned duties included helping graduate and undergraduate students with writing problems and ensuring that papers were properly formatted. The standards demanded by professors for their course papers were uniformly high. As I surveyed the faculty, however, I learned that formats for documentation varied widely. In use at the time were at least four different styles: the *Chicago Manual of Style* (Turabian), American Psychological Association (APA), Modern Language Association (MLA), and Library of Congress. The disparity made my task more difficult, because before I could help a student, I had to know which professor the paper was intended for and what style that professor was currently requiring. And consider the poor student taking four classes under four different professors, each requiring a different documentation style for course papers! Standardization had never seemed more important. That's when I convinced the dean to establish one required style for the college. The job became easier for students and faculty alike.

Many U.S. Government agencies follow the guidelines established by the *Government Printing Office Style Manual*. Some—the Central Intelligence Agency and Defense Intelligence Agency, to name only two—have their own style guides, unique to their organizations. In a perfect world, all government agencies would adhere to the same guidance regarding capitalization, punctuation, abbreviations, and other considerations of style and usage. That is not the case in our government.

It is my hope that this book will meet the needs of intelligence and national security professionals as well as students pursuing courses of study leading to those professions. If I can make your job just a little easier, and make your written products more readable, then my work is complete.

James Major

Part I

WRITING AND THINKING AS AN INTELLIGENCE ANALYST

1

The Basic Tools of Writing

> Writing is easy. All you do is stare at a blank sheet of
> paper until drops of blood form on your forehead.
>
> —Gene Fowler

The profession of intelligence demands that we be able to disseminate a usable product to the people who need it. The utility of our intelligence products depends upon basic principles such as clarity and coherence. If you have ever heard a commander or a decisionmaker complain about the usefulness of a written intelligence product, then you know why these principles are important.

As Gene Fowler aptly expresses in the epigraph above, writing requires enormous effort. No magic formula can help you write better without expending that effort. But many books teach writing as a process that can be learned, primarily through practice.[1] If your writing skills are simply rusty because you have been away from the academic environment for a number of years, then you can refresh your memory and hone those skills by doing a little reading beforehand.

It is not my intent in this guide to repeat material covered in other sources available to the intelligence analyst. In this chapter, however, I review the fundamental principles of all writing: clarity, conciseness, correctness, appropriateness, completeness, and coherence. Know and heed those principles in your written work.

Clarity

> Don't write merely to be understood. Write so you cannot possibly be misunderstood.
>
> —Robert Louis Stevenson

Follow R. L. Stevenson's advice and your readers will have few problems with your written products. What is crystal clear to you, though, may be unintelligible to a reader without your experience or background. One person's "simple" is another person's "huh?" Have someone else read your writing—a classmate, your spouse, or a friend. Actively seek constructive and objective criticism. If you cannot have a second set of eyes on your work, reread it yourself after setting it aside for a while. Read it aloud. Try hard to be objective, and read it as though you have no prior knowledge of the subject. Ask yourself, as often as possible, while you read: "Is this clear? Does it make sense?"

Below are samples of papers from intelligence analyst writing. (The remarks in parentheses are mine.) Did these intelligence analysts reread what they had written?

- "I found, by using of color slides or vu-graphs that shows a madrid of activity and explaining what to look for and why it is important to be useful." (I found little to be useful in that sentence, which shows myriad—not madrid—errors and a total lack of clarity.)
- "Peters uses rescaled range analysis to study the fractal properties of time-domain behavior of stock market parameters." (You don't say?)
- "Coordinating actions and attacks leads to the other question raised by the original one but is directly tied to the first part." (Why force the reader to decipher such a complex sentence?)

Intelligence analysts are not the only ones who occasionally lack clarity in their writing. Read what a legal counsel wrote in a memo to military personnel, explaining the impact of new taxes being imposed on moving expenses:

> Any cash payment for travel or moving expenses which is not spent on an expense which would have been deductible if the member had to pay it himself, is taxable income. . . . Even better, all taxpayers will be able to exclude from income all moving expenses paid by their employers either directly or by reimbursement, if the expense would have been deductible if the taxpayer had to pay it himself, unless the taxpayer actually deducted the expense in a prior year. (Ready to do your taxes now?)

We could cite many other examples of similarly convoluted sentences and phrases from our collection. The point is this: In academic and intelligence writing, clarity is crucial. If the writing is not clear, the reader will be lost. If that reader is your supervisor or a professor scoring your midterm or research paper, you may have lost more than your credibility. So be reader-friendly. Be clear in your writing.

Conciseness

> If you would be pungent, be brief; for it is with words as with sunbeams. The more they are condensed, the deeper they burn.
>
> —Robert Southey

Blaise Pascal once apologized to a friend for writing such a long letter, but said he lacked the time to make it shorter. How true it is. A great deal of work is involved in achieving concise writing, but that work will prove its worth in your readers' satisfaction with your writing.

Don't confuse conciseness with brevity. Some long pieces of writing are nonetheless concise because they say what needs to be said without repeating; then they quit. Being concise means saying what you need to say in as few words as possible. Prune the deadwood from your phrases and sentences. Cut unneeded verbiage from paragraphs. Be merciless. Look at the phrases that follow (all from intelligence analyst papers). The italicized portions are deadwood, unnecessary to the meaning of the sentence. They do nothing but fill white space and waste the reader's time. Avoid the use of these and similar phrases in your own writing.

"the month of February"   *"the city of* Munich"   *"the* 1980–81 *period"*
"a distance of 20 miles"   "whether *or not"*   "at *the hour of* noon"

The writing example below illustrates clearly that this intelligence analyst had no concern for conciseness. Parenthetically after the example, I have included a rewrite. Compare the two and see if you think the point is still made in the shorter version.

> What has been the impact of the tax cuts on the average U.S. citizen, myself included? Although not an expert in this field, I will attempt to answer this question in subsequent paragraphs. In as few words as possible, I feel that very little was gained by the tax cuts. (The impact of tax cuts on the average U.S. citizen has been minimal.)

That 50-word dissertation on tax cuts falls into a common trap: repeating the question and overstating the obvious. We had asked intelligence analysts to write a brief essay on the impact of then-President Ronald Reagan's tax cuts. Many writers start out answering a question by simply rephrasing or repeating it. That is the old trick of trying to use as many pages in the examination blue book as possible, to impress the professor or supervisor with your depth of knowledge. But the supervisors know the questions they have asked, and they do not need them parroted. If anything, do some redefinition of the problem, restating the question in another form—the form in which you intend to answer it—and do it concisely.

Earlier in this chapter I suggested that you read your work aloud as a means of checking for clarity. If you find yourself pausing midsentence to take a breath, you can be sure that the sentence is too long. Long sentences—25 words or more, in general—often violate more than one principle of writing, but most importantly, they are rarely clear and, by definition, they are not concise. Look at the 79-word sentence that follows, an excerpt from a literature review.

> Frolov's article, which is based primarily on writings of the PLA leadership, demonstrates the urgency behind China's military progression, fully lending support to the hypothesis regarding a reactionary "jolt" of reality after the Gulf War, the war in which anything and everything demonstrated by the U.S. was in real time, multiple generations ahead of the then planned future of the PLA, and thus represented what the Chinese have come to call the new threat landscape, the "hi-tech war."

Did you understand the sentence after reading it only once? If you took a deep breath before beginning, you might have read it aloud without inhaling.[2] I found myself reading and rereading the sentence, trying to grasp the meaning the intelligence analyst had intended. The sentence shifts its focus from the People's Liberation Army (PLA) leadership to a Chinese "awakening" to the Gulf War to high technology employed by the United States in that war. A reader's mind must make those shifts, too. As you revise your own writing, remember: Keep your sentences comfortably concise.

Correctness

> The difference between the right word and the nearly right word is the same as that between lightning and the lightning bug.
>
> —Mark Twain

You may write the clearest, most concise, coherent, appropriate, and complete paper ever to flow from a pen or a word processor—but if it is not correct, you will offend your supervisor. I could devote a separate guide to this principle alone, but I hope the brief summary here will help you avoid some of the most common pitfalls.

Correctness in both academic and intelligence writing has two facets: factual precision and mechanical correctness. They complement each other by providing an edge of finesse that makes one person's writing better than another's.

Precision

Precision is a hallmark of the intelligence profession. The term itself is synonymous with accuracy and exactness. Say precisely what you mean. Check your facts to be sure they are facts and, if possible, that you have evidence from more than one source. Go for the lightning. If you are writing about the FIZZLE fighter and no one in the Intelligence Community has any idea of the aircraft's combat radius, do not write: "The FIZZLE is believed to have a substantial combat radius." What in the wide world of wonder does that mean? Instead, make a positive and precise statement for your reader: "The combat radius of the FIZZLE is unknown."

It's no sin to admit an intelligence gap. The most serious intelligence gap is the space between writers' ears when they try to cover up a dearth of knowledge by "writing around it." By admitting to the unknown, we may get someone's attention and initiate some seriously needed collection action. Your work might make a positive contribution by calling someone's attention to an intelligence gap of possible consequence.

Choosing the Strongest Verbs

One way to strengthen the precision of your writing is to focus on the verbs. Remember that verbs carry the action in a sentence. The stronger and more precise the verb, the more likely it is that the sentence will be meaningful.

Some verbs are vague and should be avoided. Examples include address, explore, review, show, examine, cover, discover, identify, look at, demonstrate, discuss, and investigate. More appropriate verbs such as compare, contrast, assess, measure, and evaluate can clarify what you intend to do. Moreover, they will define and shape your argument and your analytical strategy. The following are some examples of imprecise verbs used in sentences:

- A descriptive methodology will be used to *explain* the existing system.
- I will *examine* complaints about the United States.
- I will begin to *explore* potential changes in structure.
- I will *discuss* the controversy of the soldier-statesman versus the pure military professional.
- I will utilize a descriptive research methodology for the purposes of defining and *exploring* my research question.
- [T]his study will predominantly *investigate* future systems.
- Explanations will be used to *see* why the ethnic Russians in these states are important.
- Through the "snowball" technique, relevant titles listed in the bibliographies/notes of the aforementioned sources have been *discovered*.
- The conclusive phase of research will be to "*tweak*" the data gathered.

The sentences that follow, on the other hand, show the writers' attention to using more precise verbs:

- I will *compare* the number of economic intelligence requirements and their priorities since 1947 (in five-year increments) to ongoing international events and economic issues during that period.
- By *evaluating* risks and benefits in the context of the new challenges facing defense, it will be possible to determine if a more active role is required for intelligence in the formulation of defense policy.
- I anticipate drawing conclusions from this *comparative analysis* in each of the four areas measured.
- I will use a historical research approach to *assess* the current communist situation in the Philippines and to provide an

overall view of the way the communists have operated in the past.

- I will *compare* the domestic politics of Syria and Iraq [to] show how internal concerns influence the foreign policies of both nations.
- This paper *contrasts* the service viewpoints of intelligence support to information operations.

Here are three more examples of intelligence analysts' writing that suggest a lack of attention to precision:

- "Rising out of the ashes of World War II came the sphinx of communism." (Mixing its metaphors as it rose, no doubt. The *phoenix* rose, not the sphinx.)
- "Russian environmental minister Danilov-Danilyan reported that of Russia's arable land, half is unsuitable for agriculture." (Dictionaries define "arable" as *suitable* for agriculture. Did this intelligence analyst try to use a word he didn't understand?)
- "On 1 June 1992, the U.S. Strategic Command's Joint Intelligence Center (STRATJIC) was formally established from the ruminants of the 544th Intelligence Wing." (Now *there's* something to chew on. A "ruminant" is a cud-chewing animal. Chances are that this intelligence analyst meant to say "remnants.")

Mechanical Correctness

The final touch a good writer—or a considerate intelligence analyst—adds to ensure readability is a check for mechanical correctness. Proofreading and editing involve more than "dotting *i*'s and crossing *t*'s." Proofread for correctness and edit for style. Go back over your paper from top to bottom for misspellings, errors in punctuation, agreement of subject and verb, and other common errors. If you have trouble detecting spelling errors in your own writing, welcome to the club! Most peoples tend too overlook there own misteaks. (The four errors in the previous sentence exaggeratedly illustrate that point.) Computer spell-checkers help, but in that earlier sentence, the only word that would have been flagged is the word "misteaks," even though there are three other errors in the sentence. Spell-checkers and grammar-checking programs are improving, but most still do not recognize the difference between affect and effect, between there and their, or between too, to, and two. You still need to check for usage errors.

Don't rely exclusively on these programs. Look at the following composition that I have spell-checked. According to my software, there are no spelling mistakes in these 71 words:

> Eye have a spelling checker; it came with my pea see.
> It plane lee Marx four my revue mistakes eye can knot sea.
> Iran this Poe em threw it, I'm sheer your pleased too no.
> Its let her perfect in it's weigh; my checker tolled me sew.
> Now win eye right, eye no I'm write from halo two good buy.
> Bee cause every buddy nose bye now computers dew knot lye.

Try proofing your paper by reading backwards. By scanning words out of context, your mind will catch more mistakes. It really does work. A good alternative, of course, is to have someone else proofread your paper—preferably a disinterested observer with little knowledge of your topic.

Adeptness at proofreading and editing may be acquired three ways: through practice, practice, and more practice. Try different techniques to see what works best for you. For example, proofread once from the big picture working down to the individual words: Start by checking pages for appearance; then look at the form and the format for coherence and conformity; next, read paragraphs for coherence and unity, one main idea per paragraph; look at sentences next for completeness and correctness; and finally, check individual words for usage and spelling. It will not take as long as it sounds. If you are uncomfortable with that approach, next time try it the other way around—from the words, working up to the form and format.

Some errors are more serious than others. We all misuse the most frequently abused punctuation mark, the comma. It is one thing to omit the comma before "and" in a series (experts do not agree on that one); it is quite another matter to use a comma between two complete sentences with no joining word like "and" or "but" (a comma splice).

Because of the importance of correctness in writing, chapters in this guide provide more specific information on the most troublesome aspects of correct writing. We have tried to make this guide as user-friendly as possible. If you have problems with punctuation, for example, you can readily find and study only that chapter.

The most common mistakes are misspellings and errors in usage, punctuation, and agreement of subject and verb, each discussed below.

Misspellings

Some misspellings completely change the meaning of a sentence, while others leave the reader gazing quizzically into space. Look at the three examples below, from intelligence analysts' papers. Each has a typo that is obvious to us but not to the writer or the spell-checker.

- "With this insight the commander can effectively lesson the enemy threat." (Would the enemy let us use his *lessen* plan in that case?)
- "In realty, an integrated Euroterrorist front would stand little chance of success." (Then what about some other business besides real estate? This intelligence analyst strayed from *reality*.)
- "At the operational level of war, intelligence concentrates on the collection, identification, location, and analysis of strategic and operational centers of gravy." (Pour it on! This intelligence analyst didn't appreciate the *gravity* of the situation.)

Usage

English language usage is dynamic. We use words and phrases today that were unknown to our grandparents. Even in my youth, e-mail and blogs were unheard of, and the phrase "dot-com" would have engendered only blank stares. One need only listen to today's younger generation to learn that "bad" might mean "good," that "rad" has nothing to do with nuclear radiation, and that the admonition to "chill out" does not involve refrigeration. While usage rules change over the years, the basic conventions of the language remain intact, providing a framework upon which to build "correct" writing.

The better dictionaries have usage panels. These august bodies do not lay down rules and tell the population how to write; rather, they advise on the language as it is being used. Even the experts do not always agree. (See, for example, the entry under "data" in *Merriam-Webster's Collegiate Dictionary*, 11th edition, 2003.) The most common usage errors are usually clear-cut: affect/effect, it's/its, principal/principle. These troublemakers are covered in more detail in "A Usage Glossary for Intelligence Writers," chapter 10 of this guide.

Punctuation

Punctuation is difficult. Many "grammar guides" give you 72 rules for use of the comma, tack on 144 exceptions to those rules, then tell you to use the comma any time you want your reader to pause briefly. Few writers have problems with the question mark or the period, but the comma, colon, and semicolon are bugaboos. See "Punctuation," chapter 6, for more.

Subject-Verb Agreement

If you have a singular subject, then your verb must also be singular. Writers seem to have the most problems with this principle when their subject is separated by a lot of words from its verb or when there is a vague subject. Witness the following:

- "The amount of funds available have had an enormous impact." (Because of the singular subject, "amount," the verb must be "has." The writer apparently was sidetracked by the word "funds," which is closer to the verb than is the subject.)

- "I think the issue of tax raises and cuts are clouded with too much emotion." (We think it are, too. Note that the subject is "issue," but the writer used the plural verb to match the "raises and cuts.")
- "Each of these areas were administered in a professional manner." (The singular word "each" is the subject of the sentence, not the plural "areas.")

Appropriateness

Consider your reader. You seldom know precisely who will be reading your work, but you can generally make a pretty good guess, especially in an academic environment. To help you determine whether your writing is appropriate for the intended audience, ask yourself these questions: Who will read my paper? Why will they read it? How will they use the information? It is unlikely that you will be able to answer those questions every time, but the mere act of asking them may prove useful.

The use of jargon is another important consideration in appropriateness. Jargon is a type of shorthand in speech that saves us a lot of time and effort when we deal with our peers in the same profession. But there's no place for jargon in writing intended for a more general audience. Always consider whether someone without a clear understanding of the jargon you use will read your paper. If you must use an abbreviation or acronym, that's no problem; just spell it out first, and follow it parenthetically with the abbreviation. Then, when you use the term again, use the abbreviation. If you write more than a page or so without using the term, spell it out one more time for your reader. When in doubt, spell it out.

Considering your reader and avoiding jargon will make your writing more appropriate for your intended audience. And your supervisors will appreciate your efforts on their behalf.

Completeness

The flip side of the conciseness coin is completeness in your writing. When you write concisely, you want to ensure that you have said what you need to say in as few words as possible. With completeness, you want to be sure that you have not left anything unsaid. A good prewriting tool such as a balloon map or an outline helps a great deal.[3]

Go back and review that prewriting tool and compare it to your first draft. Have you covered everything that you wanted to cover? Are your main points all there? Have you resolved all questions you have raised, either by answering them or by stating that there are still some unknowns or gaps in information? If you can answer "yes" to those questions, then your paper is probably complete.

Look at completeness from several angles. The review process we have just addressed provides a "big picture" of whether your paper is complete with respect to all the major points to be covered. But review your work thoroughly to ensure that the individual paragraphs and sentences are complete.

Look for the topic sentence in each paragraph and see if all the other sentences relate to it and complete the thought it introduced. Without substantiating evidence in the form of follow-on sentences to expand upon or clarify the assertion that the initial sentence makes, the paragraph may be incomplete. The reader will be confused if the topic sentence introduces a thought and the remainder of the paragraph fails to carry that thought to completion. It's like starting your car, revving the engine, and then just letting it idle. The engine warms up, but you don't go anywhere. Carry your search for completeness down to the individual sentence.

Coherence

The assessment additionally needs to be based on human perceptions and assessment of the problem. Combining the two above factors, the determination of terrorist responsibility may

be expedited. Monitoring of the terrorist problem must be continuous and thorough, as well.

The intelligence analyst who wrote the short paragraph above
was not thinking about coherence. At least three major ideas are
competing for the reader's attention: (1) assessing the terrorism
problem; (2) determining responsibility for terrorism; and (3)
keeping track of the problem. It may be easier to keep track of
shadowy terrorist groups than to find the main idea of that paragraph.

Think of coherence as a plan, a blueprint for logical continuity in your paragraphs. Our minds have a natural tendency to
think logically, always trying to connect pieces of information to
each other and to make sense of them in terms of our own experience. When we encounter something incoherent, our minds
immediately say "Whoa!" and shift into neutral, grinding and
crunching what we have encountered, trying to bring it into focus. When we do not understand, the inevitable result is frustration.

You do not want your supervisors or professors to be frus-
trated because you failed to follow a coherent organizational
scheme in your writing. That is why the topic sentence is so important to writing. The topic sentence, usually the first sentence
of your paragraph, says to the reader: "Welcome to a new paragraph. I'm the main idea here and I'll be your guide through the
next few sentences." Pick your controlling idea—your central assertion for each paragraph—and stick with it. When you change
controlling ideas, move to a new paragraph with a smooth transition. In that way, you will ensure more coherent writing for
your reader.

Summing Up the Basics

Having reviewed the basic tools for writing a paper, you are
ready to write. Don't be so overwhelmed with rules and regulations that you shy away from writing. Just remember those six
basic principles, and review your papers with them in mind.

Keep your writing *clear* and understandable. Be *concise*, saying only what you need to say in order to get the point across. Edit and proofread as many times as possible to ensure *correctness*. Be sure your writing is *appropriate* for your intended audience, as nearly as you can determine that audience. Check the final product to ensure that you have said everything you needed to say about the subject—that your paper is *complete*. And watch for *coherence* throughout the process, sticking to an orderly, logical procedure. Finally, use strong verbs to make your point. The next chapter puts these six principles to work for you, showing you how to use the basic tools to improve your writing as an intelligence analyst.

Notes for Chapter 1

1. See, for example, James S. Major, *Communicating with Intelligence: Writing and Briefing in the Intelligence and National Security Communities* (Lanham, MD: Scarecrow Press, 2008).

2. A synonym for "inhalation" is "inspiration." In another sense of that word, you can see that this writing is anything *but* "inspirational."

3. For more information about these prewriting tools, see chapter 4, "Prewriting: Getting Ready to Write," in Major, *Communicating with Intelligence*, 2008.

2

Using the Basic Tools

To write is to risk being shot in public.

—Marie-Henri Beyle

If you seem to have particular trouble with one or two of the principles discussed in chapter 1, spend extra time on the most troublesome. It is easy for us to tell you these things, but the proof comes when the boss tells you to write a fact sheet and have it on his desk the next morning. We can never anticipate all the variables that may occur, but we can assure you that you will have to cope with some short suspense dates and deadly deadlines in your writing. There is no magic formula for writing, and the ability to write well is not something you are born with. Although some writers seem to have a "natural" ability, most of the authors who have written anything about writing admit that it is hard work, and they have to struggle with words even after years of successful writing.

Pacing Yourself

You've probably heard the old saying: Plan your work and work your plan. That adage is worth remembering, especially when the time comes to write papers. Your best work will not be done at breakneck speed. Many bad papers were written because of poor planning by intelligence analysts who just could not complete the work on time.

You will generally have a good idea of requirements early, when your supervisor announces, for example, that he needs a study written by noon Friday. (Oops, it's Wednesday already!) Sit down *now* with your planning calendar and work backward from the due date. Starting with the date the paper is due, allow yourself at least half the time to look over, revise, and polish your first (rough) draft; then note the date you intend to have a first draft written. Build in time for research, analysis, and writing.

That "backward planning sequence" will give you a list of milestones for doing your research and writing and revising the paper. If any one milestone slips, then you know immediately that something else must "give," or that you must burn midnight oil to finish on schedule. You might jot your planning calendar down on a piece of paper. A Post-it Note affixed near your desk or word processor might be a good reminder.

The sample plan discussed above is a simple linear process with milestone dates noted. You might prefer to use a daily planner, your computer's calendar, a personal digital assistant (PDA), or another device. Just be sure that the entire spectrum of your plan is visible at the same time. You do not want to flip a page on a "page-a-day" desk calendar and be surprised by those ominous words: *"Paper due today!"*

Titles, Headings, and Subheadings: Previews of Coming Attractions

Let's imagine you are searching intelligence materials for anything relevant to your topic, "Russia and Eastern Europe in a Free-Market Economy after the Demise of Communism." You have a pile of potential sources. The first paper you come across is entitled "Russia: An Analysis." Since that title tells you nothing, you turn to the first page and find the heading "Introduction." Shaking your head in frustration, you continue to thumb through the paper and find that the only additional headings are "Background," "Discussion," "Conclusions," and "Outlook." You know by now that you will have to read a considerable amount of that paper before you know what it really covers.

The second paper you encounter is entitled "Russia and the European Community: Moving toward Economic Accommodation." Now here is something that may be of some benefit. Warily, you turn to the first page and see the heading "The Turbulent 1990s and Their Impact on the Russian Economy." With renewed faith, you thumb through the rest of the paper and find each section and subsection with a title that reflects its content. You are grateful to that writer for saving you so much time in your research, because now you need to read only those sections that apply to your topic.

As exaggerated as that scenario sounds, scores of papers are like that first one. Vague titles, headings, and subheadings show laziness on the part of the writer, and they do nothing to help the reader learn more about the paper's content. Using clear, descriptive headings is one mark of a well-written, well-packaged paper.

Title: What the Paper's All About

Repeat the title of your paper at the top of page 1, but not on any other pages. If your title extends to two lines, single space it. Type it in all capital letters, centered on the page, two double spaces down from the top margin. (Note: As used in this guide, the "top margin" means one inch down from the top edge of the page. The text of subsequent pages begins one inch down from the top of the page, at the top margin.) Use the bold feature for the title and for all headings and subheadings. The title is not a "heading" as such, so the first heading beneath a title is an A-level heading (see below). It may be followed by an epigraph (see the beginning of this chapter) or other introductory text. Begin the epigraph or text one double space beneath the title.

A-level (First) Heading: A Main Topic

This is an A-level heading:

A-LEVEL HEADING

Think of headings and subheadings in your paper as an outline. More than that, however, they should accurately and completely reflect the content of the section that follows. Do not use letters or numbers for headings in your paper. Avoid the trite heading "Introduction" as your first A-level heading. *Of course* this first section supplies introductory material, and to say so in a heading is superfluous. Be imaginative; tailor a specific, descriptive heading for your own topic. Start one double space beneath the previous text, centering the heading and typing it in uppercase letters. Use the bold feature for all headings and subheadings, but do not underline.

Begin the text one double space under the major heading. Indent each paragraph approximately one-half inch (one "tab" setting on most word processors).

B-level (Second) Subheading: A Subordinate Theme

This is an example of a B-level heading:

B-level Heading

Subheadings add a neat and well-organized appearance to your paper. They break up the monotony of the printed material and help your readers make their way through the text. The second-level, or B-level, subheading is flush with the left margin and is typed in both uppercase and lowercase letters. It is placed one double space beneath the previous line. Begin the text for this section one double space beneath the subheading. Note also that all major words in the subheading, including the first word after a colon, are capitalized.

Another B-level Subheading:
Still Subordinate to the Main Topic Above

It is technically impossible to have a single subheading. Remember: If you divide a whole (an A-level section), you will have at least two parts (two B-level sections). Be careful, though, not to overdo subheadings in a paper. Generally, a 10-page paper should have no more than three or four subheadings. In your final printing of the paper, be sure that you have no subheadings "hanging" at the bottom of a page; that is, check to see that each subheading has at least two lines of text with it. Otherwise, force the subheading onto the next page by using multiple returns or a "hard page." (See also "Widows and Orphans" below.)

C-level (Third) Subheadings

This is an example of a C-level heading:

C-level Heading

Like the others, the C-level subheading begins one double space beneath the previous line. Again, for proper organizational form, there must be at least two C-level subheadings beneath a B-level subheading. It should seldom be necessary in a paper to have more than three levels of subheadings. If you need a fourth division, your organizational style is probably too complex.

C-level Subheading Format

Note that the third level is flush with the left margin and italicized, using both uppercase and lowercase letters. There should be no punctuation at the end of the subheading. The text begins two spaces below the subheading.

The Paper Layout

Font Style and Size: The Eyes Have It

Some of the more attractive fonts are Times New Roman, New Century Schoolbook, Arial, and Helvetica. The point sizes of each are often a matter of preference—personal or supervisory. Print a page of a paper using the font style and size that you propose to use, and ask your supervisor if it is satisfactory. Usually, the eyes tend to be a capable gauge: If the reader must squint to read the print, it's too small; if the writing can be read from across the room, it's too large. Seek the happy medium.

Note: An upper-case "I" in Arial font is identical to a lower-case "l," so that the word "Illinois," for example, might look like this in Arial font: Illinois.

Marginalia: Proper Margin Settings

Most word processing software sets the margins automatically. Check the default value of your system, which will probably be one inch on all sides. That is a proper margin setting. Page numbers, centered at the bottom, may be within the margin. If you write a classified paper and use either a stamp or headers and footers for the security markings, it is acceptable for those classification markings to fall within the top and bottom margins. Adjust your classification footer, though, so that it prints below the page number.

Justification

Do not use "full" justification for your papers. That is, the right edge of the text is not required to be aligned. In fact, serious spacing problems usually result when you use a proportional font and full justification. So set your default justification to "left."

Spacing

Proper spacing adds a professional appearance to your work. The text of first drafts should be double-spaced. Notes (footnotes or endnotes) and bibliographic entries, however, are single-spaced within the entry and double-spaced between entries. See the entries at the end of each chapter and in the bibliography for more examples. Space only once after periods and colons, including those in notes and bibliographies.

Widows and Orphans

In the layout of your paper, avoid having a single line of text at the top or bottom of a page. That applies to headings and subheadings as well, which should have at least two lines of text beneath them and not be left "hanging." Word processing software usually includes a feature called "widows and orphans" or something similar. These are single lines of text that appear by themselves at the top ("widow") or at the bottom ("orphan") of a page. By setting the widow and orphan control, you can avoid that problem. This precaution does not, however, relieve you of the responsibility to proofread your paper, making sure that these single lines are not there. Word processors will often "forget" what you told them, or they will do things you never told them to. So make a quick check for yourself.

Footnotes or Endnotes

In some intelligence publications, especially estimates, a footnote may convey a sense of disagreement with a majority opinion. Participants will advance a position, and one or two organizations will have an alternative view, adding a footnote to the document to express their dissenting opinion. In *academic* work, however, footnotes or endnotes are an absolute requirement. Chapters 11 and 12 of this guide deal with some of the conventions used in citing sources. The use of either footnotes (at the bottom of the page) or endnotes (at the end of the paper) might be your choice, or your college or university may specify the form and tell you what style to use. Footnotes make it easier for your reader to find a source—by glancing at the bottom of a page rather than thumbing to the back of a paper.

Page Numbers

Number pages at the bottom center, within the margin (that is, less than one inch from the bottom of the page). A title page is unnumbered. Introductory pages such as a preface, scope note, or contents (usually unnecessary in a paper with fewer than 20 pages) are numbered consecutively, using Roman numerals. The first page of text is numbered "1," using the Arabic numeral.

Some Hints for the Content

Do not open your paper by explaining methodology. Openings such as the following are trite, and they only delay getting to the point: "The purpose of this paper is to . . ."; "This study will examine . . ."; "My paper will look at the diverse components of. . . ." Instead, come right to the point. Remember that you are writing a paper as an intelligence professional. Ask yourself this question: "What does my reader want to know about the content of my paper?" Then answer that question on the first page, in the first paragraph. For example, let us suppose that you are writing about a recent coup attempt in Panaragua. Which of the two following openings do you think your reader would rather see?

> A DESCRIPTION OF WHAT I WILL TELL YOU LATER
> The purpose of this paper is to describe the events surrounding the recent coup attempt in Panaragua. The study will enumerate the possible reasons for the abortive coup, followed by a discussion of the current situation there and a look at the military leadership. Finally, the paper will provide a forecast for the future.

ABORTIVE COUP IN PANARAGUA BREEDS
TURMOIL, UNCERTAINTY

The Christmas lull provided the perfect opportunity for the disgruntled military to try to seize power in Panaragua. At first light on 25 December, Colonel Don Ron Garstia, commander of the elite Panaraguan Paratroop Brigade, led a contingent of 1,000 to 1,500 men in an armed attack on the Presidential Palace in the capital city, Ciudad Panaragua. After almost six hours of bloody fighting, President Manuel Nowayjose announced that his body-guards had crushed the revolt and that Colonel Garstia is in custody. Conditions are unsettled, and a dusk-to-dawn curfew remains in effect as Nowayjose tightens his grip on the country.

The first example never really says much. You know that a coup was attempted in Panaragua and that it failed. You know that the country has "military leadership." Or was it the coup that had military leadership? Reread the first paragraph and you'll see that you're not really sure from this context. What else do you know? By comparing the two examples, you can see that substantially more information is contained in the second illustration.

Concluding Section: All Good Things Must End

The concluding section, which may be called a conclusion, summary, or outlook, should not introduce any new information. Whatever its purpose—to conclude, to summarize, or to look to the future—it must be based on information already presented in the discussion section of the paper. It is based largely on your own analysis of the data and your resultant findings.

Appendixes and Annexes

Extra Added Attractions

You may find it desirable to include supplementary material that does not fit appropriately into the text of your paper. For example, if you are writing about congressional oversight of intelligence, you might wish to include applicable portions of the statutes or executive orders covering that subject. Appendixes or annexes are one way to do that. An appendix, as its title suggests, is appended to a document. An annex, on the other hand, is a separate but closely-related document.

Place appendixes immediately after the body of the paper. Number the pages in sequence with the pages in the paper, not A-1 or B-1. Use sequential uppercase letters for appendix titles (A, B, C, and so forth). Place the title one double space from the top margin. Center the title, and use uppercase bold lettering.

An annex might be a good vehicle for including classified information when most of your paper is otherwise unclassified. You may then write an unclassified paper with a classified annex, handled separately. Begin page numbering with "1" on the first page of a separately handled, classified annex. Be sure to read chapters 11 and 12 of this guide, and take all necessary measures to safeguard classified material.

Appendix Format

The following is an example of an appendix heading:

APPENDIX A: EXECUTIVE ORDER 12333

Center the heading, and place it one double space from the top margin. If the title of the appendix extends more than one line, single-space it. Begin the text one double space beneath the heading. If you are including in your appendix a copy of material that has been reproduced, then you will need to type the appendix heading at the top and add the page number at the bottom center of the page. Use the same margins as the paper.

Remember to number pages in the appendix following the sequence of your paper. If the last page of your paper is page 56, then appendix A begins on page 57. The exception occurs if you have a classified annex separate from an unclassified paper, or an SCI annex separate from a collateral paper. In either of those cases, the separate annex must have a title page of its own, and you will begin numbering the pages of the annex with 1.

Additional Front Matter Options

List of Figures

Generally a list of figures is required only for a longer paper that includes graphic material. Use the following format for figures, graphs, charts, or maps, adapting it accordingly. Center the heading ("List of Figures") and place it one double space below the top margin. Use the same margins as the paper: 1-inch top, bottom, left, and right. Number the page (bottom center) with a lowercase Roman numeral. Align the right edge of page numbers, as you see in the table of contents of this book.

List of Graphics

If you use more than one type of graphic material, and that list can all be displayed on one page, call it "List of Graphics" rather than "List of Figures." Rather than devote separate pages to only a few different types of graphics, consolidate them onto one page, using separate subheadings for each type of graphic— figures, maps, and tables, for example.

Center the heading ("List of Graphics") and place it one double space below the top margin. Use the same margins as the paper: 1-inch top, bottom, left, and right. Number the page (bottom center) with a lowercase Roman numeral. Align the right edge of page numbers as shown in the table of contents of this book. Use a B-level heading for each type of graphic.

How to Handle Graphic Material
(Figures, Maps, Charts, Graphs, or Tables)

Style guides differ in how to handle graphic material. This guide offers a possible way of doing it. Be sure to consult with your supervisor or professor for guidance. The simplest way to do it— and the easiest for your reader—is to cite the source of the graphic immediately below it.

If your graphic is on a page by itself, center it on the page. If it is accompanied by text, set it off from the text with a box. Label figures immediately beneath, as follows: Figure 1. Title of Figure. One double space beneath the figure label, cite your source, including all information normally contained in a standard footnote. Use one size smaller font for the label and the source documentation than you are using in the text, to help set it apart. If either the figure label or the source documentation extends beyond one line, single space the information.

Oversized Graphics Placement

You may place the graphic anywhere on the page, depending upon its size and shape. For example, it might be placed on the right side of the page with accompanying text to the left and below it. If your graphic is four inches wide or more, center it horizontally on the page and type the text above and beneath it. Do not resume your text beneath the graphic unless you have sufficient space for at least two lines of text.

Graphics Placement, Subsequent Citation, and Author's Analysis

When a graphic is page-sized, incorporate it into the paper on a page of its own, in portrait format if its orientation is vertical, or in landscape orientation if it is horizontal on the long axis of the page. In either case, label it beneath the graphic.

In some cases you might use a graphic from a source that you have previously cited in the paper. In that case, use a "subsequent citation" format instead of a full citation. See chapter 11 for a discussion of subsequent citations.

There might be occasions when you will evaluate large quantities of material from numerous sources; in that case, construct your own chart, table, or other graphic to summarize or otherwise represent your data. If you have a graphic that you constructed from your own analysis of the subject, then cite the source as "Author's Analysis." It is still necessary to cite all sources you evaluated; that is usually done in the text accompanying the graphic.

Beyond the Form and the Format

This chapter has described some specific ways to present information in writing an intelligence paper. But beyond these basic forms is the important consideration that lies at the heart of the intelligence profession: What do intelligence analysts *do*? The next chapter covers that topic in some detail.

3

What an Intelligence
Analyst Does

Ask intelligence analysts what they do.[1] You'll probably get as many answers as the number of analysts you interview. Somewhere in each answer you might even hear the word "analyze"—like the dictionary definition that defines a word by repeating it in the definition: "An analyst analyzes." This chapter tries to deconstruct that answer by getting to the root of the question: What *does* an intelligence analyst really *do*? The perspective we take is that of a manager in the Intelligence Community whose task it is to train new analysts as they arrive on the job, fresh out of academic lives and ready for their first serving of reality.

Training New Analysts

One theme surfaces repeatedly in interviews of new analysts at the end of their first year: a desire for a manual describing how to do analysis. Managers face a daunting training burden in addition to reviewing increasing volumes of production and providing vital hand-holding services during the adjustment period. Growth has also meant a higher percentage of new managers struggling with these issues for the first time.

After attempting to cope for a while, many managers are ready to conclude that analysts are born, not made—a position that may be a bit extreme. But like the old jokes, there is good news and bad news. The bad news is that there is no substitute for experience, no mechanical formulas that an eager new hire can follow to guarantee an acceptable piece of finished intelligence. Each analyst must learn the job as all prior analysts have: by trying, falling short, and trying again. The good news is that managers can facilitate the learning process if they can do three things: communicate a sense of the mission along with the differences between intelligence writing and academic writing; describe the process of intelligence analysis in a clear, cogent fashion; and prepare fledgling analysts for early failures, providing lots of positive reinforcement and reassurance.

The First Step

The manager's first task is akin to deprogramming—undoing habits formed in 4 to 10 years of college-level work. This comes down to impressing upon the would-be intelligence analyst a sense of what the job is and a thorough discussion of the nature of intelligence writing. There are seven key concepts that the new analyst must absorb, three relating to the mission and four to intelligence writing. The supervisor must hammer (if need be) the "three missions and the four essences" into the new hire's head, or face the prospect of yet another journeyman who contributes little but eats up enormous amounts of managerial time.

Mission One: The Job Is to Make Judgments about the Future

The new analyst often has difficulty accepting the idea that we are less concerned about what actually happened than we are in determining the significance of the event for U.S. interests. Moreover, conditioned by college to search for "truth"—artistic and scientific—the new analyst is sometimes slow to believe that what people *think* is true is often more important than what is *actually* the fact. And then there is that dogged determination to get all the facts, a compulsion reinforced by the mistaken notion that our job is to know everything. The new analyst must understand that:

- Judgments will invariably be made based on incomplete and conflicting information.
- Unlike college, there are no "incompletes" given here. The analyst never has the luxury of asking the consumer to wait until additional information becomes available.
- Strange as it always sounds, our job is not so much to be right as it is to provide the best answer possible, given the time and information available.

Mission Two: We Are the Interpreters of Foreign Cultures and Alien Problems

As such, our job is to expose the logic behind the actions of a Middle East madman and to render intelligible to the general reader the motivation behind a terrorist attack on children in a grade school, for example.

Mission Three: Our Job Is to Support Decisionmakers

This is a concept that all new analysts readily accept. Indeed, for many, the prospect of being part of the policy process is one of the strongest selling points of the job. But (there is always a *but*), it is a concept that many new analysts have difficulty putting into practice, because they are confused about what constitutes support.

Many believe that if they add to the policymaker's knowledge, they have done the job. The manager must stress that the point of analysis is the interpretation of information, not its presentation. Analysts must be taught to grasp the distinction between providing answers to real problems and expanding the body of knowledge on some subject. Supporting the policymaker comes down to three related functions:

- Providing answers to specific questions, only some of which may be asked by the policymaker

- Providing a framework that allows the policymaker to understand an issue and to process new information
- Where appropriate, to warn

The Differences between Academic and Intelligence Writing

The four "essences" of intelligence writing flow directly from the three dealing with the mission. The listing below summarizes four distinct differences between academic and intelligence writing.

Academic	Intelligence
Focus on the *past*	Focus on the *future*
Written for *experts* with no responsibility to act	Written for *generalists* facing real problems
Detailed, proof-laden characterizations	*Essentials* only; meaningful
Short on *conclusions*; tends to summarize	*Begins* with *conclusions*; explores implications

Essence One: Intelligence Writing Focuses on the Future

A new analyst who was struggling to make the transition from academe captured this problem best. In college, she just gathered all the facts and "the conclusions just fell out." Many are under the misimpression that the primary goal of intelligence writing is to discover truth or set the record straight, and, as a result, the first instinct is to lay out in detail how the present situation evolved.

Managers need to impress on new analysts that, because what people believe to be true is often more important than what is true, discovery of the facts alone is insufficient for and occasionally immaterial to the real job of analysis: thinking about the future. Students become analysts when they stop thinking in terms of what happened and start thinking in terms of what the facts *mean*. Many just never seem to make this transition.

Essence Two: Intelligence Is Written for
Generalists Grappling with Real Problems

One of the hardest things for new analysts to grasp is the nature of their audience. New analysts are used to writing for professors and academics who welcome detail and who are under no obligation to do anything with the information, unlike the situation in which they now find themselves. New people are also slow to realize and often doubt another truth—that after a few months on the job they are among the most knowledgeable people in the government on a particular issue, and, for the first time in their lives, they are writing for an audience who knows less than they do. They must be taught that their new audience does not judge the value of a product by its length, devotion to detail, or complexity. Nor is a well-told tale enough. New hires need to learn that the value of a paper is proportional to its clarity, brevity, and focus on issues.

Essence Three: Intelligence Writing Is the
Art of the Meaningful Characterization

New analysts resort to "data dumps" for two basic reasons: They do not know what is important so they include everything; or they believe piling up detail is the best way to demonstrate their expertise, a lesson learned in college. The manager has to impress on the new analyst that the "art of intelligence" is identifying the important data in the mountain of detail. While reporters describe the situation, analysts characterize it by making meaningful generalizations that help the reader put events in perspective and think about them. Analysts reconcile conflicting information, isolate the principle in a sea of data, and recognize the exception that demands a reevaluation.

Essence Four: Intelligence Writing Begins with
Conclusions, Then Explores Their Implications

The idea of going beyond the evidence is new for most analysts. Academic writing rarely reaches this point; what passes for conclusions in academia is more often than not a summary of the preceding pages. In college, good students learn by design or default to focus on how situations develop and fit the evidence into intellectual constructs that are more descriptive than predictive. Managers must retrain them to think in terms of "This is the situation; these forces are at work; this is what it means."

This is a very difficult transition for many people. The other elements of intelligence writing can be learned. I am less sure about this one. It seems to go to the core of the thought process. People seem either to have the ability to do it, or they do not. Some are clearly uncomfortable with ambiguity and always seek a little more information before writing. Others draft but cannot move beyond the evidence or reach intellectual closure on an issue, perhaps because they are afraid of being wrong. In any case, the ability to think beyond the evidence and to explore the implications of a situation is the *sine qua non* of intelligence analysis.

A Framework for Analysis

In addition to driving home what the new analyst is supposed to be doing and how it differs from what he or she has done in the past, the manager needs to provide a concise and simple scheme of how to produce analysis. A "how to" diagram accomplishes a number of things. It helps reduce anxiety by giving the new hire a crutch to lean on. It starts the individual off in the right direction. It reinforces the message of the three missions and the four essences. And it gives the manager and the analyst a common vocabulary and a framework for critiquing fledgling efforts.

The production of finished intelligence can be presented as a four-step process:

- Identifying the intelligence issue within the topic
- Identifying the questions that need to be addressed
- After completing the research, identifying the two or three key points the policymaker is to take away from the paper
- Drafting, using questions to organize the paper

Step One: Identify the Intelligence Issue within an Intelligence Topic

Or, deal with the "Great Title Trap." Ask a new analyst what he is writing about and, odds are, you will get a reply along the lines of "corruption in China" or "terrorist strategy in the 21st century" or "Russian activity in the Third World." And what you get is *everything* about Russian activity in the Third World, starting with Afghanistan and proceeding through Zimbabwe.

Too often the manager must bear the responsibility for the data dump or the rambling draft that lands on his desk. The sad fact is that most new analysts really do not know what they are writing about. They are researching a title given to them—a problem compounded by the fact that most titles are constructed more with an eye to snagging the reader's interest than conveying the substance of the paper. I am convinced that more papers go wrong for this reason than any other.

The solution is to teach the analyst that the first step is to identify specifically what he or she is writing about. Introducing the concept of a difference between an intelligence topic and an intelligence issue is helpful in this regard. An intelligence *topic* is a broad question of interest, such as Russian activity in the Third World. An intelligence *issue* is a development of something new and different that narrows the topic and gives a focal point to the paper. There is a simple test: an issue phrase conveys a sense of change or movement or activity; a topic does not.

Examples may help clarify this subtle, but important, distinction. Sino-Russian relations is an intelligence topic but is not an issue. The significance of China's expanding economic relations with Russia for Western investors in China, or the implications of the Putin succession for Russian policy toward China, are issues. Sino–North Korean relations is an intelligence topic; the improvement in Russian–North Korean relations and what it means for China is an intelligence issue.

The purpose of making this fine distinction is to get the analyst to stop and think about what he is attempting to do before he attempts to do it. The new hire is not going to be able to make this distinction; the ability to identify intelligence issues is one of the things that separate the apprentice analyst from the adult of the species. It is the manager's responsibility to ensure that the analyst knows exactly what he is working on.

Step Two: Identify the Questions

An intelligence issue is still too broad to provide the new analyst much help. He needs something to guide him as he reads, files, and gathers information.

One answer is to break the intelligence issue into a series of general questions. To do this, the new analyst should be encouraged to step into the policymaker's shoes and ask himself: What do I want or need to know about this issue? The questions should flow from the intelligence issue; if they do not, the purpose of the paper is probably not clear. Using the Sino–North Korean issue as an example, a policymaker probably would want to know: Have warmer Russian–North Korean relations caused cooler Sino–North Korean relations, or is it more complicated than that? Are the Chinese concerned? What steps has Beijing taken to change the situation? Is the Chinese leadership divided on the issue? What would China like to have happen? What is Beijing doing about it? Is it working? What do the Chinese expect from the United States? The first cut at this should be a spontaneous, stream-of-consciousness exercise. The analyst can then weed and consolidate the list.

The list of questions serves to sharpen the focus of the paper. The new analyst now knows "what's in" and "what's out"—for instance, whether he needs to be concerned about Russian–North Korean economic relations. The list also tells him what he should be looking for as he reads files; once that is done, it helps him identify intelligence gaps and write requirements. Because the analyst now knows what information is relevant, it should also speed up the research and prevent the indiscriminate collection of data. The questions may change as the analyst does the actual research, but this only serves to define the paper more precisely.

As with identifying the intelligence issue, the manager will have a major input in identifying the questions, and the new analyst should be encouraged to touch base with his counterparts at the State Department, Defense Department, and elsewhere. But it is important that the analyst take the first cut and actually put the questions down on paper. The exercise furthers three goals: It gets the analyst thinking in terms of an audience, it heightens sensitivity to policy relevance, and it causes the analyst to think in terms of something besides what happened. With the questions at hand, the analyst can do the research.

Step Three: After Completing Research, Identify Two or Three Key Points

This is the most important step in the process. At this point, the task for the new analyst is to: (1) digest his research, (2) decide what he knows, and (3) put down in a short paragraph or as bullets the two or three key ideas to impress upon the reader. Point (3) is the analytical bottom line, the essence of the paper, and probably the heart of the prospects or outlook section. If an analyst cannot summarize concisely his bottom line, he has not done the analysis. If he starts to write before determining his bottom line—and hopes that the conclusions will fall out of the facts—he almost certainly will never have one.

It is, of course, a very big step from (2) what you know to (3) what it means. How do we get the analyst there? The analyst cannot get there unless he first decides what it is he knows. The manager's function, then, is to get the novice to answer explicitly—if only in his mind—the questions outlined in step two.

That done, the analyst is in a position to go beyond the evidence—to think about what the answers mean. The preferred methodology is to use questions to think the issue through, questions designed to bring out the implications of the facts. There is a set of generic questions that can be used. Having digested the research, the analyst reflects on:

- What is new, or what is being done differently?
- Why is it occurring?
- What are the goals and broader concerns of the principal actors?

- What factors influence success or failure? Are the actors aware of these factors? Do they have a strategy or program to deal with the factors?
- What are the prospects for success, and, more important, what are the implications for the actors, their broader concerns, the United States, and other countries?
- Where do the principal actors go from here?

By preaching these questions, the manager gets the analyst to focus on the "big picture." The questions cannot—must not—be answered by restating the facts. The questions get at the processes and call out for generalizations, the essence of good finished intelligence. The key points the analyst wants to impress on the reader are a distillation of this thought process. An example may help clarify this. An analyst working on the Sino–North Korean paper might ask:

- What has changed in Chinese–North Korean relations?
- Why has it changed? Is it just because North Korean–Russian relations have improved, or is there something else that accounts for both developments?
- What would Beijing like to have happen?
- Does Beijing have a strategy for achieving its goals? What factors will shape success or failure? Does Beijing appreciate these factors?
- What are China's chances of success? What happens if the Chinese succeed? If they fail? What is the U.S. stake in this? Other nations?
- Where do the Chinese go from here?

Step Four: Draft, Using Questions to Organize the Paper

The final step should be the easiest. Once the analyst knows the two or three key ideas he wants to convey, the task is to organize the material in a way that makes the points most effectively. The best papers are those that are organized into sections that address what policymakers want to know and need to know. The questions used in step three often can be used to organize the draft.

Does It Work?

Yes and no. The four-step process will not make bad analysts adequate, but it does help the learning process:

- It provides a common framework and language for managers and new hires. By helping new people think about the process of writing finished intelligence, it improves their ability to master what is an art rather than a science.
- It can be used to explain to analysts why a particular draft is deficient and offers guidance on how to fix a sick draft.
- It gets the new analyst focused on the consumer and U.S. policy questions.
- It stresses that intelligence is *interpretation* of fact, not simply *recitation* of fact.

The merits of the system outlined here aside, the manager, and especially the new manager, needs to develop his or her own plan for training analysts. The art of analysis is, or should be, second nature by the time individuals are tapped for managerial positions. It may be particularly difficult to communicate to someone just how you do it, unless you take the time to reflect on what works for you and how best to get those ideas across. A system makes the manager's job easier, it standardizes training across the unit, and it allows the manager to test different approaches in a systematic way.

Whatever system or tool a manager develops, a number of other things may make the tool useful. It is especially important to discuss the differences between academic writing and intelligence with the new analyst, and to lay out for the new hire what the manager looks for in a good piece. This personal philosophy of intelligence plants a notion that there is indeed a method in the manager's madness and that not all he or she does is managerial capriciousness. The discussion also serves to establish the standards that the manager will hold the new analyst to. Mentors are fine, but the new hire needs to know what the manager thinks.

There is no substitute for practice. The more a new hire writes, the sooner he will master intelligence writing. This has to be coupled with a careful reading of the finished product for style and organization rather than substance. The new analyst should be given examples of particularly good papers, and the manager should discuss with the novice what makes the paper exceptional.

Correctly handling the first paper is also critical. The manager should go over each of his editorial changes with the new hire, explaining clearly why each was made. This may be more guidance than the analyst wants at times, but it is an essential part of the teaching process.

Getting to the Argument

With these principles in mind—the three missions and the four essences of intelligence writing—the analyst is now prepared to tackle an essential component of writing in the community: argument. Intelligence papers should present a logical, reasoned *position* on an issue. That is the subject of the next chapter.

Note for Chapter 3

1. This chapter will be of particular interest if you work in intelligence analysis or are pursuing a course of study in that field, especially if you write or review analytical papers. The chapter is based on an article by Martin Petersen that appeared in the fall 1986 unclassified edition of *Studies in Intelligence* under the title "Managing/Teaching New Analysts." We include it here because of its importance to anyone who writes in the Intelligence Community.

4

Argument in Intelligence Writing

Dr. Solveig Brownfeld

> An argument consists of evidence presented in support of an assertion or claim that is either stated or implied.
>
> —Dorothy Seyler, *Understanding Argument*

As discussed in chapter 3, an intelligence *issue* focuses on something new and different, narrowing a topic and reflecting change, movement, or activity. When analysts write about issues, they are usually taking a stand on one side of that issue or the other. For example, earlier we cited the issue of China's expanding economic relations with Russia and the significance of those relations for Western investors in China. To *argue* that issue, an analyst might state that the expanded economic relations will have a negative impact on Westerners investing in China for the next 10 years.

Characteristics of Arguments

Argument Reflects How Humans Think

Argument is nothing new in rhetoric. In ancient Greece, citizens argued their own cases in the assemblies and law courts.

They devised arguments using the rhetorical devices of Greek philosophers—Socrates, Plato, and Aristotle—and Latin rhetoricians Quintilian and Cicero. Today's writers strengthen their writing with the same persuasive devices. The value of argument lies in the fact that it reflects how humans think. "Rhetoric was the art of persuasion, and, in their study of rhetoric, these scholars were in fact studying the human mind and the ways in which human beings acquire and process knowledge through language."[1]

When You Argue, You Take a Stand

Taking a stand means supporting an assertion that develops from your research. This is the process:

- Research your topic.
- Draw a conclusion from what you have learned.
- Transform your conclusion into an assertion.
- Write your assertion as a clear thesis statement.
- Support your thesis statement with evidence from your research.
- Convince your reader with persuasive arguments.

An argument can encompass an entire document, such as an intelligence estimate, but you will also use lines of argument within your overall argument.

Example thesis statement: War x started as a result of inadequate intelligence. You support that assertion by applying causal analysis, by reasoning from example, or by using comparison/contrast.

Argument Is Central to Intelligence Analysis

Intelligence analysis involves studying information and forming a judgment. That judgment must be supported with evidence. Intelligence analysis terms resemble those of argument: Place the bottom line up front; analyze rather than describe; make a judgment; and support your judgment with evidence.

Intelligence analysis *is* argument. It presents probable, rather than certain, truth. It suggests likely causes for a war and offers predictions without the certainty of, for example, how water is formed from hydrogen and oxygen. As Horner notes, "The fact is that we live much of our lives in the realm of probabilities. Our important decisions, both at the national level and at the professional and personal level, are, in fact based on probabilities. Such decisions are within the realm of rhetoric."[2]

Organization of an Argument

The elements of a classical argument include:

Opening—gains the reader's attention.
Background—provides the facts or history of the situation.
Definition of issues—defines terms and explains issues.
Thesis—states the proposition or particular issue that is to be proved.
Proof—supports and develops the thesis.
Refutation—answers the opposing arguments.
Conclusion—summarizes the arguments and sometimes urges the audience to action.[3]

Focus on a Thesis Statement and Its Support

Thesis and proof are essential to all arguments. If your topic is controversial, refutation also becomes important.

Thesis

Other terms for thesis include claim, conclusion, assertion, proposition, hypothesis, statement of synthesis, major core assertion, and judgment. To avoid confusion, this chapter will refer to the main idea as an assertion or a thesis statement.

Proof

Other terms for proof include support, evidence, reasons, lines of argument, strategies, methods of development, and examples. Proofs make up the largest part of the argument. This chapter favors the terms *support* or *evidence* to indicate proofs.

Refutation

The refutation concedes that counterarguments exist and then disproves them. Place the refutation after the proofs. But if the counterargument is extensive, make the refutation part of the proof.

Take Prewriting Seriously

After choosing a topic, narrow it, assert something about it, and discover evidence to support it.

Invention

Quintilian (AD 35–95), head of the Roman School of Oratory, suggested examining a topic from all sides by using questions such as the following:

- What is it?
- What is it like?
- What is it not like?
- What is its purpose?
- What is its effect?
- What caused it?
- What terms are associated with it?
- What is the meaning of those terms?[4]

"[The] unconscious mind hedges what it allows into consciousness and tries to steer the conscious mind along well-worn paths. . . . But some of this repressed information remains close to consciousness and can be recalled in various ways."[5] Cavender and Kahane suggest the following methods to coax information from memory:

- Free writing: Write down everything that comes to mind on a subject.
- Mapping: Write down your main idea and circle it. Attach to it all related thoughts until you develop a "map" of the idea.
- Brainstorming: Generate as many ideas as you can on a topic without passing judgment on any idea.
- Dialoguing: Present your ideas on a topic to another person and allow that person to question you or make comments on the topic.

Formulating a Thesis Statement

As you explore your topic, try formulating and reformulating possible thesis statements. You must assert something about your subject in order to create a thesis statement.

Example:

- Intelligence collection—a subject.
- Intelligence collection during war—a narrowed-down subject.
- Intelligence collection during war is hampered by poor coordination with allies—a subject with a predicate that asserts something about the subject.

A Thesis Statement

"Intelligence collection during war is hampered by poor coordination with allies."

This assertion is affirmable or deniable. You must now marshal evidence to support that assertion.

Consider your thesis statement an organizational tool. A question, a descriptive statement, or a statement of fact are *not* thesis statements.

The thesis statement benefits both writer and reader. It will help you organize your ideas better, add a sense of purpose to your writing, and help your reader comprehend your ideas more easily.

What Does a Good Thesis Statement Look Like?

A statement of fact or description is not a thesis statement. Note that the YES statements below all make an assertion, use key words that will lead to lines of argument, and use words of assertion such as *should* and *must*. Some of the NO statements use key words but assert nothing about the subject. Note also the intelligence focus of the YES statements.[6]

NO: This paper will attempt to redefine the roles of the Army and the Air Force in close air support. *No assertion. Some key words but not very specific. No intelligence focus.*

YES: To increase operational efficiency and realize the full potential of close air support, the Army must increase intelligence resources devoted to the close air support mission, freeing the Air Force to concentrate on other missions. *The writer makes an assertion and cites specifics on how to improve a situation, with an intelligence focus.*

NO: This paper will focus on U.S. arms sales to Saudi Arabia, the advantages and disadvantages of these sales, and the effect these sales have on U.S. and Saudi Arabian policy. *This paper will probably simply describe arms sales. Its focus is policy, not intelligence.*

YES: The U.S. Intelligence Community should monitor the sales of American-made arms to Saudi Arabia because these sales will preserve U.S. interests in the region without deploying U.S. troops, will help prevent Russian expansion, and will increase security in the Persian Gulf and the Middle East. *The assertion includes key words and specifics. The "because" statement leads into a cause/effect line of argument that supports the assertion. The focus is intelligence.*

NO: Examples from the recent past demonstrate that information is a U.S. strategic center of gravity. This paper will examine this premise and suggest ways of protecting information from the effects of our enemies. *No assertion. Few key words and specifics.*

YES: The U.S. Intelligence Community must protect its information center of gravity by A-ing, B-ing, and C-ing. *The assertion lists specifics. The writer will expand on those to support the assertion.*

Developing Support for Your Thesis Statement

Back up assertions with evidence, reasons, lines of argument, thinking strategies, methods of development, and proof. The most commonly used reasoning methods include reasoning from example, induction, division/classification, comparison/contrast, analogy, cause/effect, problem/solution, and deduction.

Reasoning from Example

Reasoning from example is a common means of persuasion in argument because it reflects how humans think and speak in their daily lives. It is based on the relationship between a general principle and a specific observation or example and can move in two directions: either general-to-specific or specific-to-general. You may reason specific-to-general and draw an inference, but you will probably present your inference as general-to-specific.

Example:

(Specific) You study the Johnson Poll, the Miller Survey, and statistics.
(General) You infer from your study that the *x* party will win the election.
(General) The *x* party will win the election because—.
(Specific) You cite the Johnson Poll, the Miller Survey, and statistics.

The opposite pattern is true of the following argument:
Example:

(General) The staff members in Division D are careless and lazy.
(Specific) Mary lost our last three reports. Bob never returns my calls. Jim missed the printing deadline.

(Specific) Mary lost our last three reports. Bob never returns my calls. Jim missed the printing deadline.
(General) Therefore, I conclude that the staff members in Division D are careless and lazy.

A paragraph with a topic sentence exemplifies general-to-specific.

Example (topic sentence italicized):

Many Americans enjoy playing musical instruments. President Clinton played a saxophone. Teenagers enjoy playing the guitar at parties. Truly musical people play the piano and sing to their own playing.

Induction

At the heart of reasoning from example (or samples) is induction. This involves making an inference from specific observations. It is human nature to infer, to draw general truths from specific instances, and to conclude uniformity from a sample. Note how facts lead to an inference:

Facts: There is the dead body of Smith.
Smith was shot in his bedroom between 11:00 p.m. and 2:00 a.m., according to the coroner.
Smith was shot by a .32 caliber pistol.
The pistol left in the bedroom contains Jones's fingerprints.
A neighbor saw Jones entering the Smith home at around 11:00 p.m. the night of Smith's death.
A coworker heard Smith and Jones arguing in Smith's office the morning of the day Smith died.
Conclusion: Jones killed Smith.[7]

Richard Fulkerson, in *Teaching the Argument in Writing*, describes the relationship between samples and generalization:

Whenever we meet people, we get a "sample" of their behavior and decide what we think about them. When we go to a restaurant, or leaf through a book, or listen to a politician for an hour, we are getting a sample. Quality control checks in industry involve sampling the product at intervals and generalizing to the whole. A scientific experiment is a sample of the behavior of elements of the universe; since we assume a uniformity in nature, a small sample (one experiment) is, in theory, logically sufficient.[8]

The most common fallacy in reasoning from example is hasty generalization. The problem occurs in the samples. They must be extensive enough, allow for exceptions, and be representative of the group from which they are drawn. Terms for introducing examples include *after all, an illustration of, even, for example, for instance, indeed, in fact, specifically,* and *to illustrate.*

Division/Classification

A common method for developing an argument is division/classification. This method allows you to break a topic down into its logical component parts and to label them accordingly. It requires the same kind of logic as creating an outline.

In order to make your division logical, you must select a single dividing principle and stick with it. Ancient logicians referred to this as *partitio.*[9] For example, if we are sorting a bushel of apples, it would be a faulty division if we divided them into green, red, and sour. Two of those adjectives refer to color, the third to taste. *Logically,* we could divide our apples by color—green, red, and yellow—or by taste—sweet, sour, and semi-sweet.

The manner in which you divide and classify may in itself constitute argument. Examples include classifying a murderer as a juvenile, a violence-prone political party as a terrorist group, or abortion as murder. "By putting a subject into a class you draw on the reader's knowledge about other members of the class on the assumption that what is true for one member of the class is also true for other members of the class."[10]

Comparison/Contrast

Comparison/contrast allows you to analyze similarities and differences between your topic (or some aspect of your topic) and something else. To generate ideas for comparison/contrast, you might ask of your topic:

- What is it like?
- What is it not like?

Comparison/contrast can persuade your reader to accept your conclusion. If your argument asserts the benefits of a particular system, program, or method, you might compare the success of its use elsewhere with the anticipated success of its use as you envision it.

Logical Comparison

For a convincing comparison/contrast, you must have a basis for comparison. In formal logic this means that the elements being compared must belong to the same class. Some rules for comparison:

- Establish the basis for the comparison.
- Choose specific points of comparison.
- Make sure that those points are relevant to your purpose.
- Make it clear to the reader what the points of comparison are.

Three Approaches to Comparison/Contrast

Your task is to compare tennis shoes with jogging shoes. The points of comparison are the same in all three methods: soles, uppers, arch supports, heels.

Block-by-block: This method is easy for the writer but confusing for the reader to understand. The dividing principle is shoe types:

1. Tennis shoes
2. Jogging shoes

First describe all the features of a tennis shoe—soles, uppers, arch supports, heels. Then describe the same features in a jogging shoe.

1. Tennis Shoes: soles, uppers, arch supports, heels
2. Jogging shoes: soles, uppers, arch supports, heels

This method is clear to the reader only if the comparison is very short.

Point-by-point: This method is difficult for the writer but makes the comparison/contrast very clear to the reader. As sports writer Shirley Povich said, "If it reads easy, it writes hard."

The dividing principle in this case is the features of athletic shoes.

1. soles
   tennis shoes—soles
   jogging shoes—soles
2. uppers
   tennis shoes—uppers
   jogging shoes—uppers
3. arch supports
   tennis shoes—arch supports
   jogging shoes—arch supports
4. heels
   tennis shoes—heels
   jogging shoes—heels

Similar-Different: This method requires careful organization on the part of the writer to make it clear to the reader.

The dividing principle is similarity/difference:

1. Similar
   soles
   uppers
2. Different
   arch supports
   heels

Terms used in comparison/contrast argument: *also, in the same way, likewise, similarly, although, and yet, but, but at the same time, despite, even so, even though, for all that, however, in contrast, in spite of, nevertheless, notwithstanding, on the contrary, on the other hand, regardless, still, though, yet.*

Analogy

Analogy, a form of comparison, involves the reasoning that if two concepts or phenomena share one similarity, they will be alike in other ways.

Example: If A is like B with regard to x, A will be like B also with regard to y.

A and B are two grocery stores. A sells birthday cards. Therefore, B will also sell birthday cards. (variable x=grocery stores; variable y=birthday cards)

However, A is a large store. B is a mom-and-pop grocery. B does not have space for birthday cards.

In a good analogy, the compared elements must share several fundamental characteristics. To develop an argument from analogy, ask: With what familiar concept or phenomenon does my topic share characteristics?

Example: You assert that unmanned aerial vehicles (UAVs) can assist in border patrol. To support your assertion, you make an analogy between the border that separates the United States from Mexico and the border that separates Germany from Denmark.

Assume that UAVs have been successfully used in border patrol between Germany and Denmark. Can the writer persuade readers that UAVs would be successful on the U.S./Mexican border? Probably not. The elements compared don't share similar fundamental characteristics. In fact, they are dissimilar in more ways than they are similar: The border between the United States and Mexico is long and vulnerable to terrorist access; the border between Germany and Denmark is small and unlikely to be an entry point for terrorists.

Cause/Effect

Cause/effect helps explain how one condition or event (cause) brings (brought) about another (effect). Typical uses include investigations of disasters, reports on why things went wrong, analyses of historical events, searches for the solution of a problem, or predictions of future events.

Causal relationships are often speculative or hypothetical. James William Johnson, in *Logic and Rhetoric*, describes the role of hypothesis in cause/effect reasoning:

> [Writers] construct a probable hypothesis or conjectured explanation. When the conjecture deals with probable reasons for present phenomena, the result is a hypothetical cause. When it anticipates the consequences of present phenomena, speculating as to probable future events, the conjecture treats a hypothetical result.[11]

Since arguments deal with probable, not certain, truth, your causal analysis will attribute causes and effects on a hypothetical basis. Causation can include clusters of potential causes and effects as well as contributing conditions and influences. You must also distinguish between direct and indirect causes.

Direct Cause

The direct cause triggers an event or is primarily responsible for it. It can be seen as the precipitating cause or the immediate cause.

Indirect Cause

Your selection of a primary indirect cause from among many potential ones may become part of your argument.

Example: What are the causes of an urban riot?

The direct causes—
A sudden heat wave? The arrest of a popular local leader? Power outage?
The indirect causes—
Closing of local businesses? Long-term unemployment? Unresolved housing issues? Ongoing orchestrated political agitation?

Cause/effect reasoning can move in several directions:

Cause to effect: The riots led to worse housing conditions.
Effect to cause: The worsened housing conditions led to looting, which caused relations with police to deteriorate.

Cause to effect to further effect: The closing of local businesses led to high unemployment, which led to riots.

Example: Matches and a flammable carpet are the direct cause of a three-alarm fire. But officials also discover indirect causes:

- Unattended children were playing with matches.
- The house was not equipped with a smoke detector.
- The children's parents were substance abusers.
- The factory where the children's parents worked had just closed.
- The children's parents could not afford a babysitter because they were both unemployed.

Your cause/effect analysis may begin with the technical aspects of the fire but develop into a sociological study of poor parenting and the negative effects of a bad environment on children.

Cause/Effect and Historical Events

Determining causes and consequences of events as they occur in the succession of time is central to intelligence writing. When you apply cause/effect reasoning to historical phenomena, you are seeking the answer to two questions:

- Why did this occur (causes)?
- What are its consequences (effects)?

Consider the case of President Kennedy's assassination in 1963. Lee Harvey Oswald assassinated President John F. Kennedy November 22, 1963. As a consequence, Lyndon B. Johnson became president. But now a whole new causal chain has formed around a competing theory—that Oswald did not act alone.

Isolating Causes

A method for isolating causes is to establish key differences. This involves using comparison/contrast in combination with cause/effect.

Example: You wish to find out why the outcome of a particular urban battle was entirely different from that of another, although the battles were quite similar.

- Compare the battles in a general way.
- Make a point-by-point comparison.
- When you discover the one point on which the two differ,
  stop.

Determine if that point constitutes the key difference to the
outcome.

Avoid Fallacies

Two common fallacies to cause/effect reasoning are *post hoc*
and forced hypothesis.

Post hoc: Just because it starts raining at the same time as
you happen to spill a cup of coffee on the floor does not mean
that the rain is the agent of your act of spilling the coffee. An
example of confusing time relationship and causation is this
humorous one on women's rights: "Women were given the
vote in 1920; since then, juvenile delinquency, dope addiction,
prostitution, and organized crime have increased alarmingly;
therefore, the granting of suffrage to women was responsible."[12]

> The *post hoc* fallacy may determine the outcome of a presidential
> election.
> President Jones elected → downturn in economy → loss of jobs →
> Jones not reelected

The arrows show a sequence of events over a 4-year span,
not causation. Usually, a president does not influence the economy. The president is simply being causally linked with events
that occurred simultaneous to his being in office.

Intense public debates on issues may center on *post hoc* fallacy. Opposing sides of an issue cite entirely different causes for
a problem.

Example: A drop in SAT scores occurs in a particular school district. Students currently taking the test had been exposed to a new method for learning how to read when they were in the first grade. The first graders scored lower on this reading method than first graders had in years past under the traditional reading method.

Opponents and supporters of the reading program are in conflict. Opponents blame the reading program for lower SAT scores. Supporters, however, point to other factors causing lower SAT scores:

- The recent influx into the district of large numbers of students for whom English is a second language.
- The new policy of having all high school students take the SAT and not just those who plan to go to college.

Forced hypothesis: The scientific hypothesis must:

- Include all known facts
- Not overemphasize any part of the evidence at the expense of the rest
- Observe the laws of probability as established by previous investigation
- Avoid logical contradictions
- Stay as simple as possible without ignoring any part of the evidence

According to Johnson, if the hypothesis violates any of these, it is a forced hypothesis.[13]

Terms used with cause/effect argument are: *accordingly, as a result, because, consequently, for this purpose, hence, otherwise, since, then, therefore, thereupon, thus, to this end, with this objective.*

Problem/Solution

A simplified variation of cause/effect is called problem/solution. Using this strategy, you must first convince the reader that you know the cause for a particular problem. You must spell out your problem in some detail. Your solution will, of course, need to develop from what you perceive to be the cause of the problem.

Example: UAVs may alleviate some of our border patrol problems.

The key words in this thesis statement foreshadow how the writer will present the argument. It will require the following:

- Definition of UAVs, pinpointing exactly which ones would be feasible for border patrol and which ones wouldn't.
- A detailed description of border patrol problems that would focus on what kinds of problems UAVs can solve and what kinds they can't.
- A description of the solution.

First you determine that z is the cause for problem x. You argue that solution y will solve problem x. You will require other lines of argument to support your assertion that y will solve x, such as general-to-specific, definition, cause/effect, comparison/contrast, and division/classification.

Using problem/solution, develop your topic by asking the following questions:[14]

- What is the problem? Why is it serious? Why must there be a change?
- Will it affect my readers? How?
- What causes the problem? Is it caused by the system or the people administering it? What then must change?
- How will the proposed solution work? How will it reduce or eliminate the problem? Will it create other problems? More serious ones?
- Is the solution practical? Has it been successful elsewhere? Is its cost acceptable?
- Are there sufficient people to implement it?
- Why might people oppose it? What other solution might they suggest? Why is the proposed solution better than any others?

Deduction

Deduction and induction function together at the core of reasoning processes. Inductive reasoning moves from the specific observation to the general statement, while deduction moves from a general statement to a particular instance. But deduction is more complex than that. Horner defines it as "reasoning from a general truth about a group to an assumption about one of its members."[15]

The Syllogism

Aristotle created the syllogism, a construct with three terms, to symbolize deductive thinking:

- a major premise—a general statement
- a minor premise—a particular statement
- a conclusion—derives from the two premises and has a *therefore* relationship to them.

This is how the syllogism works:

Major Premise: All men are mortal.
Minor Premise: Socrates is a man.
Conclusion: Therefore, Socrates is mortal.

When we reason deductively in our daily lives, we tend to use the abbreviated form of deductive argument, the shortened syllogism. A shortened syllogism can become an assertion and serve as a thesis statement: Socrates is mortal because he is a man.

To refute this argument, the reader must uncover and disprove the unstated major premise, that all men are mortal (derived from induction). See the short syllogism and its full version below:

Euthanasia is wrong because it is murder.

Major Premise—Murder is wrong.
Minor Premise—Euthanasia is murder.
Conclusion—Therefore, euthanasia is wrong.

The abbreviated deductive argument—Euthanasia is wrong because it is murder—leads to a narrower thesis: We must sponsor legislation banning euthanasia because euthanasia is murder.

The unstated major premise in the shortened syllogism is often the site of illogical arguments based on questionable or untrue assumptions.

Avoid Fallacy

Common fallacies in shortened syllogisms center on the use of questionable or untrue assumptions. These include:

- Hasty generalization—occurs when you base your inductive reasoning in the major premise on too small, or too unrepresentative, a sample.
- Shared characteristic—just because two elements share one characteristic doesn't mean they share others.

Example: Abraham Lincoln was untruthful because he was a politician.

The unstated major premise (derived from induction) is—All politicians are untruthful. The full syllogism would be like this:

Major Premise: All politicians are untruthful.
Minor Premise: Abraham Lincoln was a politician.
Conclusion: Therefore, Abraham Lincoln was untruthful.

To refute this argument, examine the inductive reasoning that led to it. Perhaps the writer drew the following inference:

Specific Observation—Richard Nixon was untruthful.
Specific Observation—Bill Clinton was untruthful.
General Statement—Therefore, all politicians are untruthful.

Once you have uncovered the unstated major premise, you may counteract it with contrary evidence:

Specific Observation—Woodrow Wilson was a very honest man.
Specific Observation—George Washington was truthful.
General Statement—Therefore, not all politicians are untruthful.

Now you have used an inductive argument to refute the unstated major premise.

The full syllogism is a valuable tool for finding and testing the unstated premise in your own argument, and for finding and refuting the illogic in the arguments of others.

Toulmin Model

The Toulmin model is an expanded version of the syllogism. It consists of three primary elements—warrant, data, and claim. These correspond to major premise, minor premise, and the conclusion of the syllogism.

- Warrant: All medical students are smart. (major premise)
- Data: Jane is a medical student. (minor premise)
- Claim: Therefore, Jane is smart. (conclusion)

The Toulmin model is more flexible than the syllogism because its structure includes secondary elements—the backing, the rebuttal, and the qualifier. These additional elements allow the writer to begin expanding on the argument.

- The backing—expands on the warrant; is characterized by the word *because*; allows you to begin developing arguments that support the warrant.
- The rebuttal—same as the refutation of classical argument; is characterized by the word *unless*; allows the writer to begin anticipating counterarguments.
- The qualifier—marks the limitation of the claim; characterized by the word *probably*.
  o Warrant: All medical students are smart.
  o Data: Jane is a medical student.
  o Claim: Therefore, Jane is smart.
  o Backing: Because you have to be smart to get into medical school.
  o Rebuttal: Unless she got in because her mother is president of the college.

You may or may not choose to apply the Toulmin model or the syllogism to your argument. But by using the reasoning methods and the central principle of argument, you can greatly improve your writing. Make an assertion and marshal evidence to prove it. Your reader will thank you for it.

Notes for Chapter 4

1. Winifred Bryan Horner, *Rhetoric in the Classical Tradition* (New York: St. Martin's Press, 1988), 1.

2. Horner, 245.

3. Horner, 233.

4. Horner, 30–32.

5. Nancy Cavender and Howard Kahane, *Argument and Persuasion: Text and Readings for Writers* (Belmont, CA: Wadsworth Publishing, 1989), 9.

6. Examples are based on those given in the *Joint Forces Staff College Style Manual*, JFSC Pub 4 (Norfolk, VA: JFSC, January 2004), 9, 12.

7. Dorothy M. Seyler, *Understanding Argument: A Text with Readings* (New York: McGraw-Hill, 1994), 10.

8. Richard Fulkerson, *Teaching the Argument in Writing* (Urbana, IL: National Council of Teachers of English, 1996), 30.

9. Examples are from Horner, 98.

10. Examples are from Horner, 98.

11. James William Johnson, *Logic and Rhetoric* (New York: Macmillan, 1962), 43.

12. Seyler, 45.

13. Johnson, 44.

14. Michael E. Adelstein and Jean G. Pival, *The Writing Commitment*, 5th ed. (Fort Worth, TX: Harcourt Brace Jovanovich, 1993), 326.

15. Homer, 138.

Part II

THE USAGE MANUAL

A Note to Users

Part II of the style guide focuses on elements of usage such as economy of words, capitalization, punctuation, and the like. The user should be aware that some usage principles vary among commands, organizations, or schools. For example, some institutions treat words such as decisionmaker as two words (the same applies to policymaker and other compound words). Although this guide treats them as one word, you should be aware of any differences at your school or organization.

Another excellent source for information about capitalization, compounding, abbreviations, and numerals is the *United States Government Printing Office Style Manual* (Washington, DC: GPO, 2000). At this writing, that book is accessible online at <www.gpoaccess.gov/stylemanual>.

5

Usage and "Abusage"

Wasted Words

Conciseness makes writing clear. It is a matter of compression rather than one of omission. Omit unnecessary words that through habit have become part of intelligence writing. One small connecting word often does the work of several. See table 5.1 for a list of possible replacement words.

Numbers

Numbers can be expressed as numerals, words, or groups of words. The guidance below should simplify your choices about which form to use and will provide a logical and consistent appearance in your writing.

Cardinal Numbers

To avoid confusion, do not use cardinal numbers side by side.

Not: In 2009, 25 new divisions were identified.
But: Twenty-five new divisions were identified in 2009.

Table 5.1. Possible Replacement Words

Instead of . . .	Try this . . .	Instead of . . .	Try this . . .
abortive coup attempt	abortive coup	absence of	no
absolutely essential	essential	acres of land	acres
acute crisis	crisis	additionally, further information	further information
adequate enough	adequate	a distance of 3,000 miles	3,000 miles
advance planning	planning	afford an opportunity	let, permit, allow
after the conclusion of	after	ahead of schedule	early
a large proportion of	many	all-time record	record
along the lines of	like	appear(s) to be	appear(s), seems
appointed to the position of	appointed	as a result of	because (of)
as well as	and	at an early date	soon
at the present time	now, currently (or omit)	because of the fact that	because
bring to an end	end		
built a new	built	by means of	by, with
close confidant	confidant	close proximity	close, near
collaborate together	collaborate	commented to the effect that	commented that
compared with	than	completely untrue	untrue, false
conduct an interview with	interview	consensus of opinion	consensus, agreement
contingent upon	depends, hinges on	continue(s) to maintain	continue(s)
cost the sum of	cost	country of Iraq	Iraq
dates back from	dates from	despite the fact that	although
divide up, off	divide	do analysis	analyze
due to the fact that	because, since	during such time as	while

each and every	each
eliminate altogether	eliminate
end result	result
entirely complete	complete
entirely new departure	departure
estimated at about	estimated at
few in number	few
final settlement	settlement
follow after	follow
foreign import	import
for the purpose of	for, to
full complement of	complement of
galvanize into action	spur, prompt
give expression to	express
has the appearance of	appears
hour of noon	noon
in addition . . . also	in addition
in an effort to determine	to determine
inasmuch as	since
in conjunction with	and, or
in order that	so
in (with) regard to	regarding, on
in short supply	scarce
in the amount of	for
in the course of	in, during, while
in the event that (of)	if
in the interim period between	between

elected to the office of	elected
end product	product, result
entirely absent	absent
entirely eliminated	eliminated
established a new	established
(to) export abroad	(to) export
final outcome	outcome, result
firm commitment	commitment
for an indefinite period	indefinitely
form a new unit	form a unit
fresh beginning	beginning
future prospect(s)	prospect(s)
general public	public
gray colored aircraft	gray aircraft
heard various requests	heard requests
important essentials	essentials
in addition to	besides, also
in a number of cases	some, sometimes
include among them	include
in connection with	in, on, about
in order to	to
in relation to	toward, to
in terms of	in, for (or omit)
in the city of Paris	in Paris
in the interest of	for
in the majority of instances	usually

(continued)

Table 5.1. (*continued*)

in the midst of	amid	in the near future	soon, shortly
in the process of fighting	fighting	in the vicinity of	near, around
in 2 years' time	in 2 years	in view of the fact that	since, because, although
just recently	recently	(is) lacking in	lacks
launch a new operation	launch an operation	link together	link
local authorities	police	located at	at
major breakthrough	breakthrough	make an assessment/ estimate of	assess/estimate (verb)
may possibly suggest	suggest, may suggest	merge together	merge
(the) month of May	May	more (or most) unique	unique
necessary (pre)requisite	(pre)requisite	never before in the past	never before
new discovery	discovery	new initiatives	initiatives
new record	record	new recruits	recruits
new renovations	renovations	not generally available everywhere	not generally available; scarce
on a few occasions	occasionally	one of the last remaining	one of the remaining
one of the purposes	one purpose	on the occasion of	when, for
on the part of	by, for, among	pare down	pare
penetrate into	penetrate	perform an analysis of	analyze
pressing for the imposition of a curfew	pressing for a curfew	previous experience	experience

prior to	before	prominent and leading	prominent
prospects for the future	prospects	provided that	if
reason is because	reason	reason why	reason
recalled back	recalled	repeat again	rrepeat
request appropriations for	ask for money, funds	retain his position	remain, stay
revert back	revert	root cause	cause
safe haven	haven	serious crisis	crisis
serve as	poor substitute for verb "to be"	skirt around	skirt, avoid
small in size	small	still remains	remains
subsequent to	after, since	substantial portion	much, large part
succeeded in defeating	defeated	sufficient consideration	enough thought
take action on the issue	act	take into (under) consideration	consider
temporary reprieve	reprieve	time and time again	repeatedly
true facts facts	facts	under active consideration	being considered
until such time as	until	usual customs	customs
valued at	wort	violent explosion	explosion
when and if	if	whether or not	whether
with reference to	on, about, concerning	with regard to	regarding, concerning
with the exception of	except, except for	with the result that	so
worst ever famine	worst famine	(the) year 2010	2010

Note also that numbers at the beginning of a sentence are spelled out.

Numbers Expressed in Figures or Words

Use figures for numbers of 10 or more. If the number is the first word of a sentence, spell it out in any case. A number less than 10 is spelled out in a sentence except for age, time, and percentages. (See the exception below, in "Combinations of Numbers.")

The job took 12 men 30 days.
Forty-three men built the bridge.
The shipment consisted of three tanks and two personnel carriers.

Combinations of Numbers

In a sentence with combinations of numbers on either side of 10, use figures for all the numbers.

The enemy attacked with about 200 men, 12 tanks, and 6 aircraft.
But: The enemy attacked with one battalion of men, nine tanks, and two aircraft.

Ordinal Numbers

An ordinal number is used to indicate order in a particular series (1st, 2d, 3d, 10th). Note the omission of *n* and *r* in *2d* and *3d*. Some word processors automatically superscript the two-letter suffixes of ordinal numerals; that is acceptable practice.

That film is the 10th in our series of diversity management training classes.
Life in the 21st century is greatly improved by technological advances.

Age

Express age as a numeral.

The general is 60. (or 60 years old, but not 60 years of age)
His grandson is 3 years old.

The colonel must be in his 60s. (No apostrophe)
The 18-year-old soldier fled. (Note the hyphens.)

Expressions of Time

Use figures for expressions of time.

Intelligence analysts remained at the National Defense Intelligence
College for 1 year.
The part-time degree completion program allows 5 years.
She completed the course in only 6 months.

Centuries

Centuries are expressed in numerals for those 10 and above
(10th century, 21st century), and spelled out for the first through
the ninth centuries. Note the lowercased word *century*. Other
principles apply as in "Numbers Expressed in Figures or Words"
and "Combinations of Numbers," above.

Few historical records exist for the first through the ninth centuries.
Prussian strategist Karl von Clausewitz lived in the late 18th and
early 19th century.
Her paper covered the period from the 9th through the 12th century.
(Combination)

Clock Time

Use the 24-hour system.

Early classes meet from 0730–1000 daily.

Dates (see also "Eras")

Use cardinal numbers and day, month, year order—often
termed the "military" date style. Spell out the month, and use
the full four-digit year (14 September 2009, not 14 Sep 09 or 14
September 09 or 14 Sep 2009). Avoid using ordinal numbers (not
July 15th, but 15 July).

Indonesia declared its independence from the Netherlands on 17 August 1945.

All signers of the peace accord had left by 7 October (not 07 October).

SFC Rock received his BA degree in August 2008 (not August, 2008).

Eras

The most common era designations are A.D. (anno Domini, "in the year of our Lord") and B.C. ("before Christ"). A.D. precedes the year; B.C. follows it.

Japan instituted the Taika Reforms in A.D. 646.
Legend has it that Romulus founded Rome in 753 B.C.

Decimals

Numbers with a decimal point are expressed in figures. For amounts less than 1.0, the decimal point is preceded by zero.

The range of that mortar is 6.5 kilometers.
The concrete in that bunker is 0.65 meter thick.

Fractions

Spell out a fraction when it stands alone, begins a sentence, or is followed by *of a* or *of an*. Use numerals when the fraction is a modifier, when fractions are mixed with whole numbers, or when spelling out the fraction would obviously be awkward. Note the use of hyphens in the examples below. Be aware also that some word processors—Microsoft Word, for example—convert figures such as 1/2 to a more stylistic ½. That is usually acceptable in your papers. If you prefer to retain the fraction in the original form (1/2), simply click on the "Undo" arrow or backspace after it converts.

Her estimate of the unit's strength was one-half his.
Two-thirds of the vehicles were inoperable.
He found one-third of a mile of wire tangled in the tracks.

But: The endurance test included a 1/2-mile run.
A marathon race is actually about 26-1/5 miles.
We need a 2½-ton truck to haul this load.
The paper is about 3/1,000 of an inch thick.

Geographic Coordinates

Express latitude first. Use a hyphen between degrees, minutes, and seconds; leave a space between latitude and longitude, with no intervening punctuation. You do not need to use the words or symbols for degrees (°), minutes ('), or seconds ("); those are understood.

The village was at 60-17-44N 135-20-16E.

Money

Express monetary values in U.S. dollars, with figures preceded by a dollar sign. If the value must be given in foreign currency, place it in parentheses after the dollar amount. The initials *U.S.* are not needed before the dollar sign unless foreign dollars could be implied. Use the word *dollars* when precise amounts are not given, and use the word *cents* for amounts less than a dollar.

The missile system cost the North Koreans nearly $50 million.
He paid about 42 cents in taxes for every dollar he earned.
The work cost the firm thousands of dollars.
The foreign firm contracted the work for $300,000 (195,000 euros).

Percentages

Use numerals for all percentages (except when they begin a sentence), and always spell out the word *percent*.

Only 1 percent of the insurgent force survived the attack.
Polls predict that 94 percent of the people will vote for the incumbent.
Sixty-one percent of the people voted for the incumbent.

Possessive Case with Numbers

Numerical expressions indicating possession require an apostrophe but not a hyphen.

> After 5 years' planning, the project was scrapped.
> Libya bought several million dollars' worth of equipment (but, $10 million worth).

Punctuation with Numbers

These examples show punctuation of numbers containing four or more digits. See chapter 6 for details on punctuation for text other than numbers.

> The war claimed 1,785,642 casualties by 1945.
> The station operated on a frequency of 1800 kHz.
> His army serial number was O98500.
> The army had captured 1,525 rebels by August.

Ranges

Express as shown in this example:

> Estimates range from $12 million to $14 million (not $12 to $14 million).

Ratios, Odds, Return

Express as shown in the following examples.

> The doctor-to-patient ratio was 1:25.
> He had a 50-50 chance of winning.
> The measure was approved by a 50-to-1 vote.

Plurals and Singulars

Acronyms and Other Combinations

Do not use an apostrophe before the s in plural acronyms, groups of digits designating decades or centuries, hyphenated letter-number combinations, nicknames and class designations of items of military equipment, or military abbreviations without periods.

the 1990s	SVERDLOV Class CGs	T-62s
MiG-29s	SS-13s KRESTA IIs	Mod-2s

Note: An abbreviation of a unit of measure has neither a period nor a plural form (1 km, 10 km; 2 NM, 30 NM). Note also that style guides remain undecided—or they disagree—about how to treat decades in the 21st century. If, for example, you refer to the years 2000–2010 as "the 2000s," it might be misread as the entire 21st century. To avoid confusion, simply write "the years 2000–2010." Clarity rules!

Agreement in Number

A verb must agree in number with the subject of its sentence, and a pronoun must agree in number with its antecedent. Most often, problems with these rules arise from long, overly complex sentences, with too many words between the subject and the verb, or from failure to recognize the proper antecedent for a pronoun. Study the examples below.

Not: The Panaraguan government, stifled by the incompetence of their bureaucrats, were slow reacting to the crisis.

But: The Panaraguan government, stifled by the incompetence of its bureaucrats, was slow reacting to the crisis.

Not: Each of the citizens were asked to vote.

But: Each of the citizens was asked to vote.

Better: Each citizen was asked to vote.

Country Names and People

A country is a sovereign state. It is a singular entity that requires a singular verb and pronoun. Use the pronoun "it" or "its" in referring to a country, not "she," "her," or "their." A country has many people, and plural verbs and pronouns are appropriate in referring to those people.

> North Korea pursues its policies tenaciously.
> The North Koreans pursue their policies tenaciously.
> The United States is an example of a representative democracy, and
>   its people cherish freedom.

Puns

A pun is a play on words wherein the words are identical or similar in sound but have sharply different meanings. Writers of intelligence papers should avoid using puns such as the following:

> The hospital ship is now operational.
> The Japanese and Chinese are oriented toward economic improve-
>   ments.
> The Islamic Revolution has catholic appeal.
> In the wake of recent killings, we urged caution.
> The soldier, who was bleeding to death, made a grave mistake.
> The equipment acquisition is geared toward force modernization.
> The officer corps uniformly spoke highly of him.
> The German intelligence analyst was on the mark with her assess-
>   ment.

6

Punctuation

The main punctuation marks are the period, the coma, the colonel, the semi-colonel, the probation mark, the catastrophe, the eclipse, the Happy Face, and the box where the person checks "yes" to receive more information. You should place these marks in your sentences at regular intervals to indicate to your reader that some kind of punctuation is occurring.[1]

—Dave Barry

Clarification and Separation

All sentences depend on punctuation for their meaning. Punctuation contributes to organization, emphasis, clarity, and exactness in written expressions. In writing, punctuation performs a function similar to inflection and facial expression in speaking.

The two main purposes of punctuation are to give clarity to written statements and to make reading easy. Keep in mind that the rules of punctuation are flexible but easily misused. Any rereading of a sentence to obtain its correct meaning is a sign that punctuation has been poorly applied or that the sentence is cumbersome. Less punctuation is required in well-constructed sentences than in poorly written ones.

Discussions of punctuation marks in this chapter are arranged alphabetically for ease of reference.

Ampersand (&)

Avoid using the ampersand (&) routinely in your formal writing as a careless substitute for "and." The ampersand is properly used in some abbreviations, without a space before or after the mark. In your formal written work, first establish the abbreviation parenthetically, as in the examples below. Common uses include R&D, S&T, TO&E, and I&W. Note that the ampersand is used only in the abbreviation, not in the text.

> Libyan research and development (R&D) programs are making rapid gains.
>
> Mr. Hughes teaches scientific and technical intelligence (S&TI) twice a year.
>
> The unit's table of organization and equipment (TO&E) needed revision.
>
> Indications and warning (I&W) courses are important components of the core curriculum.
>
> His source for the information was an article in *U.S. News & World Report.*

Apostrophes and Possessives

Harry Shaw writes about the apostrophe:

> The apostrophe ('), a mark of pronunciation and a spelling symbol, has three uses: to indicate omission of a letter or letters from words and of a figure or figures from numerals; to form the possessive (genitive) case of nouns and of certain pronouns; to indicate the plurals of letters, numerals, symbols, and certain abbreviations. . . . [Y]ou must know how to employ it correctly for each of the purposes indicated if your writing is to be immediately clear and fully understandable to readers.[2]

Acronyms and the Like

The apostrophe is not used before the *s* in the plurals of groups of letters (acronyms), hyphenated letter-number combinations, groups of digits designating decades or centuries, nicknames and class designations of military equipment, or military abbreviations without periods.

SAMs	Class CGs	SS-13s
the 1990s	T-62s	KRESTA IIs
SVERDLOVs	MiG-29s	Mod-2s

Note: Possessive forms of these terms do require apostrophes: the SAM's range; the MiG-29's design; the T-62's armor.

Compound Words

Form the possessive on the last word of a compound word, even if the compound is hyphenated. Sometimes the plural possessive can sound so awkward (as in secretaries-treasurers') that you may prefer to recast the sentence where the term is used. The ear is usually a good judge.

Singular Possessive	Plural Possessive
notary public's	notaries public's
comptroller general's	comptrollers general's
secretary-treasurer's	secretaries-treasurers'

Countries and Organized Bodies

Do not use an apostrophe after the name of a country or other organized institution ending in *s*, or after a word that is more descriptive than possessive, except when the plural does not end in *s*.

United States imports are increasing.

Congress attitudes toward enacting the law are uncertain. (This one might sound better to the ear written another way: "Congressional attitudes . . . " or "The attitudes of Congress . . . ")

New Orleans streets are busy at Mardi Gras time.
Paris suburbs teem with life.
But: The children's hospital suffered damage in the earth-
        quake.
        The women's movement led to major changes in government
        policy.

Endings of *s*, *x*, or *z*

If the singular ends in *s*, *x*, or *z*, add the apostrophe and *s* for
words of one syllable. Add only the apostrophe for words of
more than one syllable unless you expect the pronunciation of
the second *s*, *x*, or *z* sound. (See the exceptions in "Countries and
Organized Bodies," above.) It is sometimes preferable to rewrite
the sentence using an *of* phrase to avoid unpleasant sounds (see
"Piling Up Possessives," below).

Strauss's comments   the Schultzes' house
Xerxes' army   Schmitz's service
Marx's theories   Gonzalez' portfolio

Geographic Names, Company Names, and Institutions

In geographic names, company names, and institutions, follow the authentic form.

He was accredited to the Court of St. James's.
St. Peter's Square is a landmark in the Vatican.
Harpers Ferry sits beside the Shenandoah and Potomac Rivers.
Dr. Proctor attended Johns Hopkins University.

Inanimate Possessive Forms

An *of* phrase may be preferable to an apostrophe and *s* to
form the possessive of inanimate things other than those denoting time, measure, or space.

Not: A corporation's long-term capital gains are important to share-
        holders.

But: Long-term capital gains of a corporation are important to share-
holders.

Not: The bill's passage will mean higher taxes.

But: Passage of the bill will mean higher taxes.

Note: Sometimes the possessive form is preferable for inanimate objects in sentences containing numerous short prepositional phrases, particularly in lead sentences.

Not: The passage of the bill at the next session of the
legislature in mid-April will depend on Senator Framstat.

But: The bill's passage at the legislature's next session in mid-April
will depend on Senator Framstat.

"Piling Up" Possessives to Avoid Awkward Constructions

Use the *of* phrase in forming the possessive to avoid "piling
up" possessives.

Not: The committee's treasurer's report was read.

But: The report of the committee's treasurer was read.

Better: The committee's treasurer read her report.

Use the *of* phrase to form the possessive of names consisting
of several words, to avoid awkward construction.

Not: The new director of the Military Geography Division's report.

But: The report of the new director of the Military Geography Division.

Use the *of* phrase to avoid adding a possessive to a pronoun
that is already possessive.

Not: We are going to a friend of mine's office.

But: We are going to the office of a friend of mine.

Better: We are going to my friend's office.

Parallel Words and Phrases

A word standing parallel with a possessive is itself possessive in form.

Not: His work, like an accountant, is exacting.
But: His work, like an accountant's, is exacting.
Or: His work, like that of an accountant, is exacting.

Pronouns

Do not use the apostrophe to form the possessive of the relative pronoun *whose* and the personal pronouns *hers, his, theirs,
ours, yours,* and *its.*

Not: Panaragua lost it's trading partners after the embargo.
But: Panaragua lost its trading partners after the embargo.

Brackets

Brackets are used to make insertions into, or changes to, quoted
matter. For example, you may need to alter the tense of a quotation to make it correspond more smoothly with the tense of your
paper's text. Sometimes you may need to insert your own words
for clarification. In the example that follows, the bracketed
words [Global Positioning System] are used to spell out the abbreviation in the text of the quotation:

> "We are very concerned that there are reports of ongoing coopera-
> tion and support to Iraqi military forces being provided by a Rus-
> sian company that produces GPS-[Global Positioning System]
> jamming equipment," Mr. Fleischer said.

Brackets are also used to alter capitalization within quoted
material. For example, if in your paper you wanted to begin a
sentence with a word that is lowercased in the original, you
could change the first letter to uppercase by using brackets. Using the example above:

"[T]here are reports of ongoing cooperation and support to Iraqi military forces being provided by a Russian company that produces GPS [Global Positioning System]-jamming equipment," Mr. Fleischer said.

Bullets

Bullets are solid circular or square symbols used to introduce special material set off in text. In this function they can take the place of numerals or dashes and are also more eye-catching, but they should not be overused. In your papers, you will rarely use bullets except for "Key Judgments" or an "Executive Summary" at the beginning of the paper. Your supervisor or professor will usually prescribe that format if it is to be used. When in doubt, ask.

Bullets can be made in Microsoft Word by using the "Insert" menu, then clicking "Symbol" and the bullet symbol under "General Punctuation." You can also use that menu to set up a shortcut (a macro), so that a quick combination of keystrokes will produce a bullet. For example, I assigned the ALT key plus the letter "b" to produce a bullet. Alternatively, you may use a lowercase "o" as a bullet; just be sure to space once after it.

Frequently bullets are used with dashes (also called em dashes), or with double hyphens in a series of indented text blocks in which some blocks are subordinate to more important ones. For example (note the alignment):

- This is a primary statement.
  —This is a subordinate statement.
  —This is another subordinate statement.
- This is the next primary statement.

Note: Introduce blocks of text with a colon at the end of the preceding paragraph, as we have done above. Capitalize the first letter in each line of bullet and dash phrases. End each line with a period if it is a complete sentence; otherwise, no punctuation is needed. *Be consistent*: If one primary statement is a complete sentence, make them *all* complete sentences.

Colon

The colon is equivalent to "for example" or "that is." A colon may separate two main clauses when the second explains or amplifies the first. Capitalize the word immediately after a colon if what follows is a complete sentence, as in the first example.

> We stand at a great divide: We must trade or fade.
> Ann has these qualities: endurance, patience, and wit.

As follows or *the following* requires a colon if it introduces a formal list.

> In addition to Georgetown University, the following institutions belong to the Consortium of Universities of the Washington Metropolitan Area: American University, Catholic University, Gallaudet, George Mason, George Washington, Howard, Marymount, National Defense University, Southeastern, Trinity, University of the District of Columbia, and the University of Maryland College Park.

Note that the same sentence, below, is less weighty without the "as follows" and the colon:

> In addition to Georgetown University, the Consortium of Universities of the Washington Metropolitan Area includes American University, Catholic University, Gallaudet, George Mason, George Washington, Georgetown, Howard, Marymount, National Defense University, Southeastern, Trinity, University of the District of Columbia, and the University of Maryland College Park.

Never use a colon in this form:

> He bought many kinds of food, such as: cereals, fruits, nuts, and vegetables.

Do not insert a colon between a verb and its object or between a preposition and its object.

> Not: Three keys to success are: ambition, hard work, and luck.
> But: Three keys to success are ambition, hard work, and luck.

Not: Success is a combination of: ambition, hard work, and luck.
But: Success is a combination of ambition, hard work, and luck.

Comma

The comma is the most frequently used—and abused—punctuation mark. It usually performs the functions for which most punctuation is required: It separates one idea from another so that the reader can see them distinctly; it encloses incidental or parenthetical expressions; and it emphasizes certain sentence elements by setting them apart from the remainder of the sentence. Some commas are mandatory, as in a series; others are inserted at the writer's option for clarity.

To avoid misusing the comma, apply this formula: Use one comma to separate; use two commas to enclose.

Adjectives Following Nouns

Adjectives following nouns are set off by commas.

Washington's winter, snowy and cold, seemed to last forever.

Note the difference between that example and the following:

Washington's snowy and cold winter seemed to last forever.

Adverbial Modifiers

A comma usually sets off adverbial modifiers if they come at the beginning of a sentence.

When you go to the supply room, bring me some pencils.
If you call me before noon, I can meet you for lunch.

If an introductory adverbial clause or phrase is short and is unlikely to be misread, omit the comma.

On our way home we met several friends.

When such an adverbial element ends with a verb or preposition, use a comma before a following noun or pronoun to prevent misreading.

Soon after, the colonists' first settlement was started.

An adverbial modifier at the end of a sentence need not be set off unless it is long, is introduced by *although*, or needs special emphasis.

Bill will not miss the meeting if we fax him.
Kurds may still live in that region, although they are also found in other areas near the border.

Comma Splice

Avoid linking two main clauses with only a comma between them—a comma splice. Without any punctuation, it is called a fused sentence (see "Fused Sentence," below).

Comma splice: The captain attended the ceremony, the sergeant did, too.

Correct the comma splice by rewriting the sentence:

The captain attended the ceremony, and so did the sergeant.
The captain and the sergeant attended the ceremony.
Both the captain and the sergeant attended the ceremony.

Contrasting Statements

Use a comma to set off contrasting statements in a sentence.

Sharon, not Arafat, made the decision.

Coordinating Conjunctions

A comma is used before the coordinating conjunctions *and*, *but*, *for*, *so*, *yet*, *or*, and *nor* in compound sentences containing two or more main clauses but no subordinate clauses.

This sentence contains two independent clauses, and a comma is required.
Use the comma, for it can help prevent misreading.

In a simple sentence with a compound predicate, the comma
is not needed before the coordinating conjunction. Note the difference in the second example, however, where there are two independent clauses (complete sentences).

She went to Europe to study but decided not to stay.
She went to Europe to study, but she decided not to stay.

Writers often punctuate incorrectly when an adverbial
phrase begins the second part of a compound sentence. In this
case commas are used to enclose the adverbial phrase, and another comma before the conjunction *and* would be superfluous.

Stars are punctual and, by the use of a transit telescope, their passage
can be accurately noted.

Fused Sentence

Two main clauses with no punctuation between them constitute a fused or run-on sentence.

The fog was heavy the patrol could not see the bridge.

Correct the fused sentence by any of the following methods:

The fog was so heavy that the patrol could not see the bridge.
Because of heavy fog, the patrol could not see the bridge.
The fog was heavy. The patrol could not see the bridge.
The fog was heavy; the patrol could not see the bridge.
The fog was heavy, and the patrol could not see the bridge.

Introductory Prepositional Phrases

Do not separate introductory prepositional phrases unless
they deserve special emphasis, need clarification, or might lead
to misreading.

On 10 October the new rule will become effective.
In Washington the weather is usually pleasant in May.
But: In the time it takes to reload, his pistol is rendered useless.

If an introductory element is obviously parenthetical, separate it from the remainder of the sentence.

In light of this report, we must review our earlier decisions.
On the other hand, his decision may have been hasty.

Parallel Adjectives

If the order of adjectives can be reversed, or if *and* can stand between them, the adjectives are parallel and should be separated by a comma.

a hard, cold winter   a heavy winter overcoat
long, slender, brittle stems   short tributary streams

Parenthetical (Nonrestrictive) Elements

Parenthetical elements—words, phrases, or clauses—are not considered necessary to the grammatical pattern or main thought of the sentence. They are, therefore, nonrestrictive (nonessential) and are set off by commas. If the words, phrases, or clauses—all of which are termed modifiers—are essential to the meaning of the sentence, they are restrictive and should not be set off by commas.

Nonrestrictive: The new armored vehicles, which arrived yesterday, are parked in the unit's assembly area. (The clause adds information about vehicles that have already been identified. Commas are needed.)

Restrictive: A boat that leaks is of little use. (The clause *that leaks* is essential to the meaning of the sentence. No commas are needed. Use the pronoun *that* instead of *which* if the clause is restrictive.)

Participial phrases are set off by commas unless they are restrictive or used in place of a noun.

Nonrestrictive: Having his orders, he left at once.
Used as a noun: Having his orders meant he could leave at once.
Restrictive: He excused the men having orders.

Elements not needed for grammatical completeness but related to the thought of the sentence are set off in most instances by commas.

We are able, fortunately, to mail the letter on time.
Cooperation, however, was impossible.
The project, we think, is most important.
On the other hand, training should be easier.
All things being equal, I believe we will win.
There being no further discussion, the meeting was adjourned.

Series of Words, Phrases, Letters, or Numerals (the Serial Comma)

Use commas to separate a series of words, phrases, letters, or numerals. Include the comma before the word *and* as well as the word *or* in a series.

He met with the Chief of Staff, battalion commander, and platoon leaders.
Firing ranges in use today include 25C, 19D, and 15E.
We will send Joan, Jan, or Jim to the next meeting.

Transitional Words

Transitional words such as *therefore, however, moreover, nonetheless, consequently, accordingly, indeed, yet, hence, further, likewise, also,* and *otherwise* are usually set off by commas.

They will understand, therefore, why we acted as we did.
Analysts disagreed, however, with the Team Chief's assessment.

Because the demon word *however* seems to cause so many problems, take special note of the following additional examples of its punctuation.

Your supervisors will not write your papers for you, however much
you may offer them.
The teams continued to play despite the rain; however, the umpire
called the game when the lightning began.
The teams continued to play despite the rain. However, the umpire
called the game when the lightning began.
The teams continued to play despite the rain; the umpire called the
game, however, when the lightning began.
The teams continued to play despite the rain. The umpire called the
game, however, when the lightning began.

Comma after City and State Names

Always use a comma between the name of a city and its
state. State names are spelled out in the text of formal papers:

The military exercises are scheduled for July near Quantico, Virginia.
Bolling Air Force Base is situated in southeast Washington, DC. (Note
"DC," *not* "D.C.")

Use a comma after the state name in a sentence whether you
would normally pause there or not:

Near Bel Air, Maryland, we passed a convoy of tanks on the high-
way. (A pause is natural after the state name.)
The Bel Air, Maryland, traffic jam resulted from the convoy of tanks
on the interstate at rush hour. (No pause, but the comma prevents
possible misreading.)

Comma inside Quotation Marks

Always put commas inside quotation marks, even if the quotation has no comma.

"One must listen to the sound of one's prose," writes Barbara Tuchman.

Dashes

Dashes in typewritten--as opposed to composed or typeset--
material are represented by two hyphens, as shown in this sen-

tence. Two hyphens are the grammatical equivalent of an em dash. Some word processors—Microsoft Word, for example—automatically convert the two hyphens to an em dash, as shown in this sentence, when you insert a space immediately following the word after the two hyphens. When a dash falls within a sentence, leave no space before or after it. Use the dash sparingly, to mark a sudden break in thought, to emphasize a thought, or to set off a parenthetical element that is very abrupt or contains commas. Do not substitute dashes indiscriminately for other punctuation marks or for inserting a second sentence in the first.

> Japan—unlike Iran—must import vast amounts of oil.
> Italy's elite forces—the 2nd, 4th, and 5th battalions—have already deployed for the exercise.
> Worker tensions are expected to increase as a result of the second wage freeze this year—and may well prompt a strike in the next few weeks.
> Not: Our analysis indicated—We knew we were right all along—that the Republican Guards were in full retreat.
> But: Our analysis indicated that the Republican Guards were in full retreat. We knew we were right all along.

Ellipsis Periods

Ellipsis periods, also called ellipsis marks or ellipses, show that something has been left out of a quoted passage. Three spaced periods indicate that the words following them are from the same sentence. Four spaced periods are appropriate when you have omitted (a) the last part of a quoted sentence or (b) a complete sentence or more. An ellipsis is not needed at the beginning or at the end of a quotation, because it is assumed that material preceded or followed what you have extracted. Never use ellipses simply for dramatic effect.

> According to *Bartlett's Familiar Quotations*, Abraham Lincoln said, "It is true that you may fool all the people some of the time . . . but you can't fool all of the people all the time."

Note: Microsoft Word often closes the spaces between ellipses. Observe the difference between the ellipses above and below. Either form is acceptable, as long as you are consistent throughout your work.

> According to *Bartlett's Familiar Quotations,* Abraham Lincoln said, "It is true that you may fool all the people some of the time...but you can't fool all of the people all the time."

The examples below use the following quotation as their basis. Refer back to this quotation as you review each sample.

> "President Bush yesterday called on Russia's government to investigate and halt arms shipments to Iraq from Russian companies. Mr. Bush said in a telephone conversation with Russian President Vladimir Putin that his government should investigate and stop military assistance to Iraq," White House spokesman Ari Fleischer said. "We are very concerned that there are reports of ongoing cooperation and support to Iraqi military forces being provided by a Russian company that produces GPS-jamming equipment," Mr. Fleischer said.[3]
> "President Bush yesterday called on Russia's government to . . . halt arms shipments to Iraq from Russian companies. Mr. Bush said in a telephone conversation with Russian President Vladimir Putin that his government should investigate and stop military assistance to Iraq," White House spokesman Ari Fleischer said. (Here you have omitted a few words in the first sentence and stopped your quotation early.)

Four periods are appropriate in some instances. Note the spacing of the ellipses in the examples that follow, and compare the quoted portion to the original. Quoted portions in each case again come from the paragraph quoted earlier.

- Omitting the last part of a quoted sentence:

> "President Bush yesterday called on Russia's government to investigate and halt arms shipments to Iraq from Russian companies. Mr. Bush said in a telephone conversation with Russian President Vladimir Putin that his government should investigate and stop military assistance to Iraq." . . ."We are very concerned that there are

reports of ongoing cooperation and support to Iraqi military forces being provided by a Russian company that produces GPS-jamming equipment," Mr. Fleischer said. (Note the omitted words at the end of the sentence, the space after "Iraq," and then the spaced ellipses.)

- Omitting the first part of a quoted sentence:

"President Bush yesterday called on Russia's government to investigate and halt arms shipments to Iraq from Russian companies. Mr. Bush said in a telephone conversation with Russian President Vladimir Putin that his government should investigate and stop military assistance to Iraq," White House spokesman Ari Fleischer said. . . ." [T]here are reports of ongoing cooperation and support to Iraqi military forces being provided by a Russian company that produces GPS-jamming equipment," Mr. Fleischer said. (Note the period at the end of the second sentence, with no space after "said," and then the three spaced ellipses. The bracketed letter T shows that you changed the case of the original, from lowercase to uppercase.)

- Omitting a complete sentence or more:

"President Bush yesterday called on Russia's government to investigate and halt arms shipments to Iraq from Russian companies." . . . "We are very concerned that there are reports of ongoing cooperation and support to Iraqi military forces being provided by a Russian company that produces GPS-jamming equipment," Mr. Fleischer said. (Note the omitted sentence and the punctuation. There is no space between "companies" and the period; then the three ellipses are evenly spaced.)

Remember that ellipses are *not necessary* at the beginning or at the end of a quotation, because it is usually understood that you have omitted material before and after that which you have quoted.

Hyphen

The hyphen has many and varied uses. Hyphenate words chiefly to express an idea of unity or to avoid ambiguity.

Adverbs and Adjectives Ending in *-ly*

No hyphen is necessary for adverbs ending in *-ly* and preceding a participle or adjective.

> The countries of the former Soviet Union have poorly developed economies.

Adjectives ending in *-ly* are another matter:

> Ambassador Sko is a gravelly-voiced, grizzly-maned statesman of the old school of diplomacy.

Avoiding Ambiguity

It is clear that no first use policy applies in that case. (Is it really clear? Note the difference between "no first-use policy" and "no-first-use policy." Not only is clarity at stake here but also the meaning of the sentence.)

> President Bush will speak to a group of small business owners from Pennsylvania. (Since he would not likely be speaking to altitudinally disadvantaged people, "small-business owners" would be correct.)

Hyphens are also used to distinguish a compound from a word of a different meaning, such as re-creation from recreation, re-form from reform, and re-sort from resort, and to avoid difficulty in reading, as in tie-in instead of the vowel-laden tiein.

Compound Words (Unit Modifiers)

Common compound words usually are not hyphenated when the first element is a prefix (subconscious, predestination, antiterrorism, counternarcotics, postnasal) or when the last element is a suffix (breakup, blowout).

Use a hyphen when a compound adjective precedes a noun, in a prepositional-phrase compound noun consisting of three or more words, or when a prefix is added to an existing compound. Hyphens are not used in the term *Commander in Chief*.

Sino-Soviet relations appeared to have improved by the 1980s.
The infantrymen fought valiantly in the winter-spring campaign.
The icebreaker is seeking a south-southwest transit of the straits.
Former President Nuñez-Santiago heads the government-in-exile.
Intelligence requirements are complex in the post-9/11 era.
The exercise included non-U.S. NATO forces.

Use a hyphen when an adjective or noun is prefixed to a noun with the suffix -ed, as in double-faced, or when an adjective is followed by a present participle, such as sinister-looking.

Doubling or Tripling Letters (Avoidance of)

A hyphen is usually used when a letter would otherwise be doubled or tripled in combination, as in anti-inflation and hull-less. Notable exceptions are cooperate, coordinate, nonnuclear, and preempt.

E-Words

Use a hyphen with words derived from the sense of "electronic," as in e-commerce (electronic commerce), e-mail (electronic mail), and e-zine (electronic magazine). Do not overuse these trendy words in your formal writing, though.

Ex-, Self-, Well-, and Other Prefixes

Always use a hyphen with the prefixes *self-* and *ex-*: self-determination, ex-dictator. Compound words with prefixes such as *well-, better-, best-,* and *ill-* take the hyphen before a noun, unless the expression has another modifier (as in "exceptionally well suited to be an analyst"). Consult your dictionary if you have any doubts.

Well-maintained equipment can help keep a soldier alive in combat.
But: That unit's equipment is not well maintained.
The better-written paper earns the higher grade in academic work.
But: Her paper was better written than his.

Single Letters Joined to Other Words

Use a hyphen to join a single letter to a noun or a participle. (See also "E-Words," above.)

A-frame	D-Day	E-Bonds
H-hour	I-beam	R-rated
T-shaped	U-boat	X-ray

Suspensive Hyphens

Suspensive hyphens are a useful device, as in the following examples. Note the space after the first hyphen.

The A- and H-bombs exploded harmlessly in the desert.
The intelligence analyst included both pre- and post-test results in her thesis.
The 15- and 18-meter-long platforms can be disassembled.

Titles

Do not hyphenate a civilian or military title denoting a single office, as in Commander in Chief, Secretary General, Vice President; but use a hyphen with a double title like secretary-treasurer. As the last element of a title, the adjectives "elect" and "designate" require a hyphen: president-elect, vice president-elect, and ambassador-designate.

To help you decide whether to hyphenate a word or expression, see the list of troublesome words in chapter 9, "Compounding and Other Troublemakers."

Italics or Underlining

Modern printers and word processors support italics; if yours does not, use underlining instead. Never mix the two, though. Underlining in typewritten material is the equivalent of italics. Italicizing helps differentiate or give greater prominence to letters, words, and phrases. Italicize (underline) material sparingly to avoid excessive use, thus defeating your purpose. Avoid using italics or underlining for emphasis. Whenever this book refers to italics, consider underlining as the alternative.

Aircraft and Ship Names

Italicize the proper names (not types or classes) of aircraft, spacecraft, ships, submarines, and artificial satellites. Do not underline or italicize the abbreviations SS, USS, or HMS.

flight of the *Spirit of St. Louis*	USS *Wisconsin*
seizure of the *Pueblo*	the shuttle *Enterprise*
the USS *Constitution's* hull	*TIROS III*

Distinctive Letters, Words, or Phrases

Italicize to distinguish letters, words, or phrases from the remainder of the sentence, so that the reader can quickly comprehend the thought. It may also be helpful to use bolding.

The word *impact* is vague and much overused.
The supervisor used the letter *L* to signify that an intelligence analyst had been late with a paper.

Quoted Words in a Series

A profusion of quotation marks spoils the appearance of a printed page. Use italics instead.

Not: Use carefully such descriptive words as "considerate," "cooperative," "well-poised," "cheerful," and "assertive."

But: Use carefully such descriptive words as *considerate, cooperative, well-poised, cheerful,* and *assertive.*

Foreign Words and Phrases

Italicize, but do not translate, foreign words and expressions that are non-Anglicized but familiar to American readers or easily understood because of their similarity to English.

> *sputnik* diplomacy   advocates of *democracia*
> *party aktiv*   *persona non grata*

Note: When a non-Anglicized or unfamiliar foreign word appears in ordinary text, italicize it and follow it with a translation, interpretation, or explanation in parentheses. Italicize the translation only if it is the title of a publication, as in the second example below.

> the achievement of *enosis* (union)
> Jakarta *Merdeka* (*Freedom*)

For most foreign titles, an explanation is more relevant and useful than a literal translation.

> *Merdeka*, the official Indonesian newspaper, . . .

If a translation is given, it should be italicized (or underlined) and in parentheses. No translation is needed for such familiar titles as *Frankfurter Allgemeine Zeitung*, *Pravda*, *Trud*, *Der Spiegel*, *Stern*, and *Izvestiya*.

Do not italicize the original language or English translation of names of foreign organizations, institutes, governmental bodies, political parties, educational institutions, economic enterprises, corporations, and so forth. The English translation, in parentheses, should follow the foreign-language name. Here again, an explanation of the name or description of the organization can be more useful than a translation.

> The story was reported by Novosti, the Soviet press agency.

Titles of Books and Periodicals

Italicize book and periodical titles.

> For her review, she read Christopher Andrew's *For the President's Eyes Only*.
> According to an article from the *Baltimore Sun*, peace talks were suspended.
> *National Geographic* is a widely read journal.

Parentheses

Parentheses, like pairs of dashes, enclose explanatory comments or asides not intended to be part of the main thought. This usage has the advantages of simplifying sentences that would otherwise be encumbered with unwieldy subordinate and coordinate clauses, and of permitting the use of pointed asides that might seem overemphatic. A disadvantage is the possible loss of the thread of grammatical sequence, especially if the parenthetical matter is long or contains many details. Like other stylistic devices, parentheses can be overused. Keep in mind that words within parentheses can be considered "throwaway" material, thereby having the effect of weakening your writing.

Do not insert a second complete sentence parenthetically into an original sentence, as in "President Mubarak met with King Hussein (the two leaders had not met since last April) on 4 February." Instead, make two sentences or change the parenthetical material into a phrase, as shown in the following examples.

> President Mubarak met with King Hussein on 4 February. The two leaders had not met since last April.
> President Mubarak met with King Hussein on 4 February; the two leaders had not met since last April.
> President Mubarak met with King Hussein on 4 February, for the first time since last April.

Use parentheses in the text of your paper to enclose an abbreviation or acronym after you have spelled it out. Use the abbreviation thereafter.

> Her thesis covered problems with intelligence support to special operations forces (SOF). In the Army, SOF include Rangers and Special Forces.

Period

The period brings the reader to a full stop at the end of a sentence. This is its primary function. Other uses are discussed and illustrated in chapter 8, "Abbreviations." Space only once after a period at the end of a sentence.

Note: Military style omits periods in most abbreviations:

> NATO leaders met at the UN to discuss events in former republics of the USSR.

A notable exception is the abbreviation for the United States: U.S.

Adding a period at the end of a sentence that already has a form of terminal punctuation is superfluous, as in the following examples:

> Stalin's daughter defected to the U.S.

(No second period is needed. As a general rule in this case, though, it is preferred not to end a sentence with an abbreviation.)

> The key question in his hypothesis was: "How will budget cuts affect the Intelligence Community?"

(No additional punctuation is necessary after the question mark.)

Question Mark

Direct Query

Use a question mark for a direct query:

> "Can the North Koreans produce chemical weapons?"

No question mark is needed for an indirect query, which is actually a declarative sentence:

> "The general asked whether the North Koreans could produce chemical weapons."

Rhetorical Questions

A rhetorical question is one that is asked without expectation of an answer. You cannot expect your reader to answer a question you have posed in your writing. Intelligence writing should answer questions, not ask them.

Quotation Marks

Block Quotations

Block quotations consist of four lines or more of text that you have quoted directly from a source. Because a block quotation is indented and single-spaced, its form shows that it is quoted, so quotation marks are not used to enclose it. If, however, there is quoted material within your block quotation, enclose that material in double quotation marks.

Double and Single Quotation Marks

Quotation marks come in pairs and in two forms: double and single. The latter never appears unless the former is present. That is, single quotes are used to enclose a quotation within a quotation, as in the examples below. In the first two sentences, the only difference is the spacing of the quotation marks after the word agreement. Note that the second example, with a space between the closing single and double quotation marks, is more attractive to the eye—and less likely to cause confusion.

> Jim said, "I used the term 'gentlemen's agreement.'"
> Jim said, "I used the term 'gentlemen's agreement.' "
> Joan asked, "Why call it a 'gentlemen's agreement'?"

Article Titles

Quotation marks are used for titles of magazine and journal articles. Book titles are not enclosed by quotation marks (except in messages) but are underlined or italicized.

Army intelligence analyst Major Ronnie Ford wrote an article entitled "General Westmoreland and the Khe Sanh Test" for the May
1999 issue of *Army* magazine.

Punctuating with Quotation Marks

In using other punctuation marks with quoted words,
phrases, or sentences, follow these rules:

At the end of quoted material, periods and commas are always inside
the quotation marks.
Dashes, colons, and semicolons are always outside quotation marks.
Question marks and exclamation points are placed inside the quotation marks when they apply to the quoted matter only; outside
when they refer to the whole sentence.

Semicolon

The semicolon is almost equal to a full stop; in this usage it can
be likened to a "supercomma" or a "semiperiod." Do not use a
semicolon when a comma will serve; do not omit one when it
should be used. Semicolons are often incorrectly substituted for
colons, although their functions are quite different: The semicolon is a mark of separation, the colon a mark of anticipation.
Space only once after a semicolon.

Conjunctive Adverbs

Use a semicolon before conjunctive adverbs (therefore, however, hence, thus, consequently, accordingly, further, moreover,
nevertheless, and so forth) when they connect two complete and
related thoughts. (Also see "Transitional Words," under Comma.)

The director publicly commended us for our report; however, he
later asked us to rewrite the conclusion.
The new system will be operational Monday; therefore, we need the
instructions by Friday.

Independent Clauses

If independent clauses (complete sentences) are not joined by a comma and coordinating conjunction (and, but, or, nor, for, so, yet), a semicolon can be used in place of the missing conjunction and comma, as in the second example below. All three ways of punctuating the sentence below are acceptable. It is a matter of choice and style.

> Order your supplies today, because tomorrow may be too late.
> Order your supplies today; tomorrow may be too late.
> Order your supplies today. Tomorrow may be too late.

Series of Clauses or Phrases

To avoid misreading, use semicolons to separate the members of a series when the items themselves contain commas.

> The following parties gained seats in the National Assembly: Socialist, 37; Republican, 7; Communist, 3.
>
> Not: Accompanying the admiral to the contract award briefing were Mrs. Lewis, the CEO of Crabtree Pyrotechnics, General Payne, the commander of the military district headquarters and the Celebration Committee chairman. (How many people attended the briefing?)
>
> But: Accompanying the admiral to the contract award briefing were Mrs. Lewis; the CEO of Crabtree Pyrotechnics; General Payne, the commander of the military district headquarters; and the Celebration Committee chairman.

Virgule

The virgule (also called the diagonal, separatrix, shilling mark, slant, slash, or solidus) should be used sparingly and never in place of the hyphen or dash. In particular, the phrase *and/or* is greatly overused in government writing. The virgule is used as shown in the examples below.

- To represent *a*, *an*, or *per* in abbreviations: km/h (kilometers per hour).
- To separate alternatives (avoid this vague usage in your writing): program/budget decision; examine and/or analyze.
- To separate elements in numerical expressions, such as messages: CS9919/120430Z Jun 84.
- In fractions: 2/3, 4/5.
- To separate official and nickname designations of foreign aircraft or versions of aircraft: MiG-29/FULCRUM; Su-17/ FITTER-D/H.
- In some Russian and Chinese airfield designations: Xian/ Lintong Airfield.

A virgule is often used to represent September 11, 2001, as in the expression "9/11." Such a usage is acceptable in your work as a change of pace from using the full date every time; but don't overuse it.

Notes for Chapter 6

1. Dave Barry, *Classic Dave Barry Calendar* (Kansas City, MO: Andrews McMeel, 2008), April 5/6.

2. Harry Shaw, *Punctuate It Right!* (New York: Harper & Row, Publishers, 1963), 37.

3. Bill Gertz, "Bush Pressures Putin to Stop Arms Sales," *Washington Times*, 25 March 2003, A1.

7

Capitalization

Two Principles

Two main principles govern the use of capitals: Proper nouns, titles, and first words are in uppercase letters; common nouns are in lowercase unless they have gained the status of proper nouns. These principles are discussed in greater detail below.

Coined Names

A coined name or short form for a military, economic, political, or other grouping is capitalized. *Note:* Standards differ on capitalizing these terms.

the Alliance (for NATO)	the Free World
the Arab World	the Greens
the Blue Knights	the Intelligence Community
the Cold War	the Middle East
the Third World	the West (political bloc)
the Far East	Western Hemisphere

Derivatives of Proper Names

Capitalize proper nouns that have become associated with a development by their originator.

Bailey bridge	Machiavellian
Reaganomics	neo-Stalinism
Gaullist policies	Patton tank

Common Nouns in Proper Names

A common noun used alone as a well-known short form of a specific name is lowercased.

the basin (Caribbean Basin)	the heights (Golan Heights)
the canal (Panama or Suez Canal)	the isthmus (Isthmus of Panama)
the gulf (Persian Gulf)	the river (Rhine River)

Titles Preceding a Name

Capitalize an official title immediately preceding a person's name or the title of a top official previously identified by name. Any cabinet or command-element military position should be capitalized. Do not capitalize the word *former* or the prefix *ex-* in front of a title, unless it is the first word of a sentence.

former Chancellor Kohl; the ex-Chancellor	former PLO Chairman Arafat
DIA Director LTG Maples; the Director	Republican Party Chairman
former President Reagan; the ex-President	former Prime Minister Gandhi
Secretary of Defense Gates; the Secretary	the Vice Chief of Staff
Queen Elizabeth; the Queen	the Defense Minister

President Bush; the President   Colonel Jones;
            the Colonel

Titles Following or Replacing a Name

Lowercase formal titles of lower-level government and military officials when not identified by name. Lowercase terms that are job descriptions rather than formal titles.

the Australian Army commander the presidency
a general   presidential assistant
party boss Krenz   Russian leader Putin

Governmental Bodies

Capitalize the proper name of a national governmental body (U.S. or foreign).

the British Commonwealth; the Commonwealth
the British Parliament; Parliament
the Colombian Congress; the Congress; but the Colombian legislature; the legislature
the Japanese Diet; the House of Councilors; the House of Representatives
the National Security Council; the Cabinet
the U.S. Government; the French and German Governments; but the national government; the Kohl government; the communist government; the government
Note: the Bush administration

Political Parties and Philosophies

Capitalize the official name of a political party. Lowercase the indirect reference.

communist; anticommunist movement; communism; socialism; anti-
communism
the Communist Party of the United States; the Politburo; the Central
Committee; the party; a communist ideology; a socialist platform
the Labour Party; labour goals
a Democrat, Republican, Socialist, Liberal, Tory (party members)

Diplomatic Units and Corps

Capitalize the proper name of an embassy and mission. Uppercase titles of key personnel.

the British Embassy; the embassy
the Japanese Ambassador; the Ambassador
the Chargé d'Affaires; the Chargé
the Foreign Ministry; the Ministry
the Foreign Minister; the Minister
the French Consulate; the consulate
the Pakistani Consul General
the U.S. Defense Attaché
the U.S. Mission; the mission

Historic Events

Events that have gained status owing to a widely recognized development are capitalized.

the Cold War; post-Cold War   the Great Leap Forward
the Cultural Revolution   the Islamic Revolution

Titles of Publications

Capitalize all principal words of publication titles. Key words
are nouns, pronouns, verbs, adjectives, adverbs, and parts of
compounds that would be capitalized standing alone. Many
newspaper and magazine article titles are printed using lower-

case letters. When referring to such a title in the text of your paper, standardize the capitalization. Do not capitalize (except as the first word of the title or subtitle) the articles *a*, *an*, and *the*; the prepositions *at*, *by*, *for*, *in*, *of*, *on*, *to*, and *up*; the conjunctions *and*, *as*, *but*, *if*, *or*, and *nor*; or the second element of a compound numeral (Twenty-seven intelligence analysts). When writing a headline that contains an infinitive, do not capitalize the *to*.

> U.S. Persian Gulf Interests: A Historical Perspective
> A Proposal to Build a Reconnaissance Technical Facility in Korea
> Zen and the Art of Intelligence Analysis
> Marines to Receive New Equipment

Military-Associated Terms

Capitalize the full proper name (or translation) of a military entity, whether U.S. or foreign. Lowercase an indirect or general reference.

> the Defense Intelligence Agency; the agency; but, defense intelligence
> the French Army; the army (indirect or general)
> the Israeli Defense Forces
> the Joint Staff
> the Royal Air Force; the air force
> the Russian Armed Forces; the armed forces; ground forces; naval forces; air forces
> the Strategic Rocket Forces
> the U.S. Air Force; the Air Force; but, the air forces (indirect, often plural)
> the U.S. armed services; armed forces; military services
> the U.S. Army; the Army; but, the army (indirect or general)
> the U.S. Marine Corps; the Marines (the Corps); but marines (individuals)
> the U.S. Navy; the Navy; but, the navy or the navies (indirect or general)

Shortened forms of names of individual units, however, are not capitalized.

the 2d Army; the army
the 2d Battalion; the battalion
the 4th Infantry Brigade; the brigade
the 7th Fleet; the fleet

For Emphasis

Do not capitalize the first letter of a word just to stress it, and avoid uppercasing whole words or sentences for emphasis—a common technique in e-mails. To set off a word or phrase, italicize (or underline) it, but use this device sparingly.

Military Designators

The lack of standard policy for capitalizing major items of military equipment, both communist and noncommunist, has caused considerable variance in its application to products. Use the following for guidance.

Free-World Ship Classes

The class names of ships produced by Free-World countries are set in capital and lowercase letters, and are not italicized.

Hamburg Class (destroyer)
Polaris Class (submarine)

Military Exercises and Operations

Names assigned to military exercises or operations are uppercased, but not the word *operation*. Thus:

Our unit spearheaded operation DESERT WATCH.

The same principle applies to the word exercise.

operation NORTHERN WATCH
operation DESERT STORM
operation IRAQI FREEDOM

operation PEACE FOR GALILEE
exercise GRAINY HIDE
exercise TEAM SPIRIT-04

NATO Nicknames

NATO-designated nicknames for aircraft, ships, and weapon systems produced by former Warsaw Pact nations, Albania, and former Yugoslavia, as well as Asian Communist countries, will be set in uppercase, even if they are being used by Free-World countries. In referring to classes of ships, the word *Class* should follow the uppercase name on first appearance in the text, but it can be dropped in later references. See the examples that follow.

BLACKJACK-A (bomber variant)
Ka-27/HELIX (helicopter)
KNIFE REST (radar)
KASHIN Class (destroyer)
KIEV Class (carrier)

Mi-24/HIND (helicopter)
SA-3 (GOA) (missile)
YANKEE Class (submarine)
KRESTA II Class (cruiser)
SHANGHAI Class (patrol boat)

Other Named Equipment

Except for acronyms and NATO nicknames, names of other major items of military equipment produced by communist and Free-World countries are set in capitals and lowercase. These items include aircraft, missile systems, radars, manned and un-manned spacecraft and space systems, tanks, vehicles, and artillery.

Alouette III (helicopter)
Cosmos-1452 (satellite)

McDonnell Douglas F-15 (fighter)
Nike Hercules (surface-to-air missile)

8

Abbreviations

General Policy

Use abbreviations sparingly and only when you are certain the reader will understand what they represent. Too many abbreviations in the text make reading and understanding difficult. When you use the shortened form, spell out words and phrases in full on their first appearance, followed by the appropriate abbreviation in parentheses. For example:

> The budget for the Department of Defense (DoD) increased last year.

Note that military style omits periods and spaces in acronyms. At the end of this chapter is a list of frequently encountered abbreviations.

To prevent misreading, do not end a sentence with an abbreviation. Note how the following two sentences might be misread:

> Deployments pose continuing challenges for the U.S. Army Reserve troops are being mobilized.

Spell out "United States" in this case.

Abbreviations to Avoid

Latin Abbreviations

Avoid using the Latin abbreviations *e.g.* and *i.e.* Their meanings are often misunderstood and therefore misused. Instead, write "for example" and "that is," in each case followed by a comma. Another Latin abbreviation to avoid is *etc.* (and so forth), because it, too, is frequently misused—especially at the end of a series of items following "for example." See chapter 11 for the use of secondary citations instead of Latin abbreviations such as *ibid.*, *et al.*, and *op. cit.*

Measure

Do not abbreviate a unit of measure used in a general or approximate (dataless) sense.

> Ranges are given in kilometers. (Not: Ranges are given in km.)
> The crater was several meters wide. (Not: The crater was several m wide.)
> But: The missile has a range of 3,000 km.
> The 3,000-km-range missile malfunctioned on liftoff.

Months and Days

Do not abbreviate months and days. Use a full military date style: 15 January 2005, not January 15, 2005, 15 Jan 05, 15 January 05, or 15 Jan 2005.

Country Names

Except for a few well-known cases, the names of countries are generally not abbreviated at first reference. Repeated reference to countries with long names calls for abbreviation.

UK, UN

These abbreviations, without periods, are acceptable as adjectives or, preceded by *the*, as nouns. *British* is also acceptable as an adjectival alternative for UK.

U.S.

In the abbreviation for the United States (U.S.), use periods. As a general rule, abbreviate when U.S. is used as an adjective, and spell it out when it is used as a noun:

> The U.S. Government is studying the differences between the positions of France and the United States.

USSR

To save space, USSR is not spelled out.[1] For variation, substitute the Soviet Union (or the former Soviet Union). FSU is an accepted abbreviation for the former Soviet Union. Use USSR as an adjective only for government councils and ministries (USSR Council of Ministers, USSR Ministry of Agriculture). Otherwise, the appropriate adjective is Soviet. Russia or Russian refers to the state itself, the specific ethnic group, or the language; do not use the term as a synonym for USSR or Soviet.

The Two Germanys

These former countries might be referred to in historical references as East Germany (German Democratic Republic, GDR, or the East German Government) and West Germany (Federal Republic of Germany, FRG, or Bonn).

The Two Koreas

When referencing the two countries, use South Korea (or Seoul) and North Korea (or Pyongyang).

UAE

The United Arab Emirates should be abbreviated. Do not use the term *Emirian* as an adjective for the UAE.

Foreign Terms

Spell out the name of a foreign agency or institution in English, if possible, but use the common abbreviation even if it is formed from the foreign wording. For example:

Committee for State Security (KGB)

Incomplete or Possessive References

Avoid wording that puts an abbreviation immediately after an incomplete or possessive form of the name abbreviated.

Not: the Liberal Democratic Party's (LDP) platform
But: the platform of the Liberal Democratic Party (LDP)

Plural Forms

If an abbreviation's first appearance in the text is plural, the abbreviation also must be in the plural form even though the singular is used thereafter: armored personnel carriers (APCs).

Sometimes an abbreviation not ending in *s* is nevertheless plural, as in Strategic Arms Limitation Talks (SALT). The negotiating sessions at Geneva are abbreviated SALT I and SALT II.

Military Grades with Abbreviations

The *Government Printing Office Style Manual* is a good reference for these and other abbreviations. *Note:* Not all military ranks shown in table 8.1 are still in use.

Table 8.1.   Abbreviations of Military Grades

Army Officers	Army Noncommissioned Officers and Enlisted
General O-10, GEN	Sergeant Major of the Army, SMA
Lieutenant General O-9, LTG	Command Sergeant
Major General O-8, MG	Major E-9, CSM
Brigadier General O-7, BG	Sergeant Major E-9, SGM
Colonel O-6, COL	First Sergeant E-8, 1SG
Lieutenant Colonel O-5, LTC	Master Sergeant E-8, MSG
Major O-4, MAJ	Sergeant First Class E-7, SFC
Captain O-3, CPT	Specialist Seven E-7, SP7
First Lieutenant O-2, 1LT	Platoon Sergeant E-7, PSG
Second Lieutenant O-1, 2LT	Staff Sergeant E-6, SSG
Chief Warrant Officer Four, CW4	Specialist Six E-6, SP6
Chief Warrant Officer Three, CW3	Sergeant E-5, SGT
Chief Warrant Officer Two, CW2	Specialist Five E-5, SP5
Warrant Officer, WO	Corporal E-4, CPL
	Specialist Four E-4, SP4
	Private First Class E-3, PFC
	Private E-2 / E1, PV2 / PVT
Navy and Coast Guard Officers	*Navy and Coast Guard Enlisted[2]*
Admiral O-10, ADM	Master Chief Communications
Vice Admiral O-9, VADM	Technician E-9, CTCM
Rear Admiral (Upper half) O-8, RADM	Senior Chief Communications
Rear Admiral (Lower half) O-7, RDML	Technician E-8, CTCS
Commodore O-7, COMO (wartime only)	Chief Communications
Captain O-6, CAPT	Technician E-7, CTC
Commander O-5, CDR	Communications Technician
Lieutenant Commander O-4, LCDR	First Class E-6, CT1
Lieutenant O-3, LT	Communications Technician
Lieutenant (junior grade) O-2, LTJG	Second Class E-5, CT2
Ensign O-1, ENS	Communications Technician
Chief Warrant Officer W-2, 3, 4,	Third Class E-4, CT3
CWO-2/-3/-4	Seaman E-3, SN
Warrant Officer, WO	Seaman Apprentice E-2, SA
	Seaman Recruit E-1, SR
Air Force Officers	*Air Force NCOs and Enlisted*
General O-10, Gen	Chief Master Sergeant of the
Lieutenant General O-9, Lt Gen	Air Force, CMSAF
Major General O-8, Maj Gen	Chief Master Sergeant E-9, CMSgt

(*continued*)

Table 8.1. (*continued*)

Air Force Officers	Air Force NCOs and Enlisted
Brigadier General O-7, Brig Gen	Senior Master Sergeant E-8, SMSgt
Colonel O-6, Col	Master Sergeant E-7, MSgt
Lieutenant Colonel O-5, Lt Col	Technical Sergeant E-6, TSgt
Major O-4, Maj	Staff Sergeant E-5, SSgt
Captain O-3, Capt	Sergeant E-4, Sgt
First Lieutenant O-2, 1st Lt	Senior Airman E-4, SrA
Second Lieutenant O-1, 2nd Lt	Airman First Class E-3, A1C
	Airman E-2, Amn
	Basic Airman E-1, AB
Marine Corps Officers	*Marine Corps NCOs and Enlisted*
General O-10, Gen	Sergeant Major of the Marine Corps,Sgt Maj
Lieutenant General O-9, Lt Gen	Sergeant Major E-9, Sgt Maj
Major General O-8, Maj Gen	Master Gunnery Sergeant E-9 MGySgt
Brigadier General O-7, BGen	First Sergeant E-8, 1stSgt
Colonel O-6, Col	Master Sergeant E-8, MSgt
Lieutenant Colonel O-5, Lt Col	Gunnery Sergeant E-7, GySgt
Major O-4, Maj	Staff Sergeant E-6, SSgt
Captain O-3, Capt	Sergeant E-5, Sgt
First Lieutenant O-2, 1st Lt	Corporal E-4, Cpl
Second Lieutenant O-1, 2nd Lt	Lance Corporal E-3, LCpl
Chief Warrant Officer W2, 3, 4, CWO-2, CWO-3, CWO-4	Private First Class E-2, PF
Warrant Officer, WO	Private E-1, Pvt

State, Province, Territory, and District Names

In footnote and bibliography entries, use the U.S. Postal Service two-letter abbreviation, without periods, for states, provinces, territories, and the District of Columbia.[3] Do not abbreviate the names, however, in the text of your papers. The abbreviations are found in table 8.2.

Table 8.2.   Two-Letter State Abbreviations

AL	Alabama	NH	New Hampshire
AK	Alaska	NJ	New Jersey
AZ	Arizona	NM	New Mexico
AR	Arkansas	NY	New York
CA	California	NC	North Carolina
CO	Colorado	ND	North Dakota
CT	Connecticut	OH	Ohio
DE	Delaware	OK	Oklahoma
FL	Florida	OR	Oregon
GA	Georgia	PA	Pennsylvania
HI	Hawaii	RI	Rhode Island
ID	Idah	SC	South Carolina
IL	Illinois	SD	South Dakota
IN	Indianae	TN	Tennessee
IA	Iowa	TX	Texas
KS	Kansas	UT	Utah
KY	Kentucky	VT	Vermont
LA	Louisiana	VA	Virginia
ME	Maine	WA	Washington
MD	Maryland	WV	West Virginia
MA	Massachusetts	WI	Wisconsin
MI	Michigan	WY	Wyoming
MN	Minnesota	CZ	Canal Zone
MS	Mississippi	DC	District of
MO	Missouri		Columbia
MT	Montana		
GU	Guam	GU	Guam
NE	Nebraska	PR	Puerto Rico
NV	Nevada	VI	Virgin Islands

Abbreviations Often Found in Research

Table 8.3 is a list of abbreviations commonly encountered in books and journals. Many organizations and institutions now follow *The Chicago Manual of Style* (15th ed.) by discouraging Latin abbreviations such as *e.g.*, *i.e.*, and *etc.* It is likely, however, that you will still see these abbreviations in works

Table 8.3. Abbreviations Often Found in Research

anon.	anonymous
bk., bks.	book(s)
c., ca.	circa: "about"; for approximate dates (c. 1884, ca.1884)
cf.	confer: "compare"; not a synonym for *see*
chap., ch., chs.	chapter(s)
col., cols.	column(s)
comp.	compiler, compiled, compiled by
ed., eds.	editor(s), edition(s), or edited by
e.g.	*exempli gratia:* "for example"
et seq.	*et sequens:* "and the following" (or ff., which is shorter)
ex.	example
f., ff.	and the following page(s) (pp. 79f. or pp. 79ff.)
fig., figs.	figure(s)
ibid.	*ibidem:* "in the same place as quoted above"; refers to title in footnote immediately above; author's name not given; page given if different from the one preceding
i.e.	*id est:* "that is"; preceded by a comma and followed by a comma and list or explanation
ill., illus.	illustration; illustrated by
l., ll.	line(s)
loc. cit.	loco citato: "in the place cited"; refers to work fully identified in any previous footnote except the one immediately preceding; preceded by author's last name; no page number, because *loc. cit.* means "in the same location" (page) as in last footnote referring to that source
MS, MSS	manuscript(s); always capitalized; no periods
N.B.	nota bene: "take notice; mark well"; always capitalized
n.d.	no date given
no., nos.	number(s)
n.p.	no place of publication (or no publisher) given
op. cit.	*opere citato:* "in the work cited"; preceded by author's last name, followed by page number since op. cit. stands for title only; refers to work cited previously but not immediately above
p., pp.	page(s)
passim	"throughout the work, here and there"; (p. 37 *et passim* means page 37 and other scattered pages; or pp. 37-42 *passim*)
pl., pls.	plate(s)

pseud.	pseudonym, pen name (Lewis Carroll or Mark Twain, for example)
pt.	part
q.v.	quod vide: "which see"
rev.	revised or revised by; revision; reviewed by
rpt.	reprint
sc.	scene
sec., secs.	section(s)
sic	"thus"; not an abbreviation, but often encountered; used within brackets to indicate that an error in quoted material was in the original: "It was to [*sic*] bad."
s.v.	*sub verbo:* "under the word"
tr., trans.	translator, translation, translated by
v., vv.	verse(s)
viz.	*videlicet:* "namely"; used with or without a period; usage varies
vol., vols.	volume(s); 9 vols.; capitalized only before Roman numeral: Vol. VII

you use for research, so it is important that you know their meanings.

If you find other terms that are not included here, consult your dictionary. Our list is adapted from Roberta H. Markman, Peter T. Markman, and Marie L. Waddell, *10 Steps in Writing the Research Paper* (New York: Barron's Educational Series, 1989, 144–45).

Abbreviations Often Found in Intelligence Publications

Table 8.4 comprises abbreviations commonly found in intelligence products. It has been compiled largely from authorized abbreviation lists of the armed services and other government agencies. Use abbreviations only when you are certain your reader will understand them or when lack of space in a table or on a graphic makes their use necessary. Generally, they should not be used in the text. Those that may be used in the text should

(text concluded on p. 135)

Table 8.4. Common Abbreviations and Acronyms

Alphabetically by Full Name	
Full Name	*Abbreviation*
academic year	AY
airborne command post	ABNCP
Airborne Warning and Control System	AWACS
air defense artillery	ADA
air defense zone	ADZ
air-launched cruise missile	ALCM
air order of battle	AOB
air-to-air missile	AAM
air-to-surface missile	ASM
air warning; all-weather; automatic weapon	AW
amplitude modulation	AM
antiaircraft	AA
antiaircraft artillery	AAA
antiballistic missile	ABM
antimissile missile	AMM
antisatellite	ASAT
antisubmarine warfare	ASW
antitank guided missile	ATGM
armored personnel carrier	APC
Association of Southeast Asian Nations	ASEAN
battalion	BN
battery	btry
biological warfare	BW
calendar year	CY
centimeter(s)	cm
chemical, biological, and radiological	CBR
chemical warfare	CW
circular error probable	CEP
command and staff exercise	CSX
command, control, and communications	C3 or C^3
command post	CP
command post exercise	CPX
Committee for State Security (former Soviet)	KGB
communications exercise	COMEX
communications intelligence	COMINT
communications satellite	COMSAT
communications security	COMSEC
Communist Party of the Soviet Union	CPSU
Conference on Disarmament in Europe	CDE
Coordinating Committee	COCOM
Council for Mutual Economic Assistance	CEMA

Alphabetically by Full Name	
Full Name	Abbreviation
defense attaché	DATT
demilitarized zone	DMZ
Department of Defense (Note the lower-case "o")	DoD
direction finding	DF
electronic warfare; early warning	EW
electronic countermeasures	ECM
electronic counter-countermeasures	ECCM
electronic intelligence	ELINT
electro-optical intelligence	ELECTRO-OPTINT
enhanced radiation weapon	ERW
European Community	EC
European Economic Community	EEC
extremely low frequency	ELF
field artillery	FA
field training exercise	FTX
fiscal year	FY
foreign instrumentation signals intelligence	FISINT
Foreign Liaison Office	FLO
former Soviet Union	FSU
forward edge of the battle area	FEBA
forward line of troops	FLOT
free rocket over ground	FROG
general headquarters	GHq
(Soviet) General Staff Intelligence Organization	GRU
Greenwich Mean Time	GMT
gross domestic product	GDP
gross national product	GNP
ground-controlled approach	GCA
ground-controlled intercept	GCI
ground-launched cruise missile	GLCM
ground order of battle	GOB
Gulf Cooperation Council; Government Control Center	GCC
high explosive	HE
high-explosive antitank	HEAT
high frequency	HF
human resources intelligence	HUMINT
identification, friend or foe	IFF
imagery intelligence	IMINT
Improved-Homing-All-the-Way Killer	I-HAWK
indications and warning	I&W
infrared; Intelligence Information Report	IR

(*continued*)

Table 8.4. (*continued*)

Alphabetically by Full Name	
Full Name	*Abbreviation*
initial operational capability	IOC
Intelligence Information Report; imaging infrared	IIR
intercontinental ballistic missile	ICBM
intermediate-range ballistic missile	IRBM
Intermediate-range Nuclear Force	INF
International Monetary Fund	IMF
Israeli Defense Force	IDF
Japan Defense Agency	JDA
Japanese Self Defense Force	JSDF
kilogram; kilograms	kg
kilometer; kilometers	km
kilometers/hour	km/h
kiloton; kilotons	kt
kilovolt; kilovolts	kV
kilowatt; kilowatts	kW
knot; knots	kn
laser intelligence	LASINT
Lebanese Armed Forces	LAF
line(s) of communication	LOC(s)
liquid oxygen	LOX
Long-Range Aviation	LRA
low frequency	LF
measurement and signature intelligence	MASINT
medium-range ballistic missile	MRBM
military district	MD
military region	MR
Military Transport Aviation (Soviet)	VTA
millimeter; millimeters	mm
missile order of battle; main operating base	MOB
Multinational Force	MNF
multiple independently-targetable reentry vehicle (warheads)	MIRV
nautical mile	NM
naval order of battle	NOB
Nonaligned Movement	NAM
noncommissioned officer	NCO
Non-Soviet Warsaw Pact	NSWP
North Atlantic Treaty Organization	NATO
nuclear intelligence	NUCINT
Official News Agency of the Former Soviet Union	TASS
open-source intelligence	OSINT

(continued)

Table 8.4. (*continued*)

Alphabetically by Full Name	
Full Name	*Abbreviation*
Theater Nuclear Forces	TNF
transporter-erector-launcher	TEL
transporter-erector-launcher and radar	TELAR
ultrahigh frequency	UHF
under construction	UC
unidentified	UI
Union of Soviet Socialist Republics	USSR
United Kingdom	UK
United Nations	UN
United States	U.S.
unmanned aerial vehicle	UAV
vertical/short takeoff and landing	V/STOL
vertical takeoff and landing	VTOL
very high frequency	VHF
very low frequency	VLF
Warsaw Pact	WP
Watch Condition	WATCHCON

Alphabetically by Abbreviation	
Abbreviation	*Full Name*
AA	antiaircraft
AAA	antiaircraft artillery
AAM	air-to-air missile
ABM	antiballistic missile
ABNCP	airborne command post
ADA	air defense artillery
ADZ	air defense zone
ALCM	air-launched cruise missile
AM	amplitude modulation
AMM	antimissile missile
AOB	air order of battle
APC	armored personnel carrier
ASAT	antisatellite
ASEAN	Association of Southeast Asian Nations
ASM	air-to-surface missile
ASW	antisubmarine warfare
ATGM	antitank guided missile
AW	air warning; all-weather; automatic weapon
AWACS	Airborne Warning and Control System
AY	academic year

Alphabetically by Abbreviation	
Abbreviation	Full Name
BN	battalion
btry	battery
BW	biological warfare
C3 or C³	command, control, and communications
CBR	chemical, biological, and radiological
CDE	Conference on Disarmament in Europe
CEMA	Council for Mutual Economic Assistance
CEP	circular error probable
cm	centimeter; centimeters
COCOM	Coordinating Committee
COMEX	communications exercise
COMINT	communications intelligence
COMSAT	communications satellite
COMSEC	communications security
CP	command post
CPSU	Communist Party of the Soviet Union
CPX	command post exercise
CSX	command and staff exercise
CW	chemical warfare
CY	calendar year
DATT	defense attaché
DF	direction finding
DMZ	demilitarized zone
DoD (Note the lower-case "o")	Department of Defense
EC	European Community
ECCM	electronic counter-countermeasures
ECM	electronic countermeasures
EEC	European Economic Community
ELECTRO-OPTINT	electro-optical intelligence
ELF	extremely low frequency
ELINT	electronic intelligence
ERW	enhanced radiation weapon
EW	electronic warfare; early warning
FA	field artillery
FEBA	forward edge of the battle area
FISINT	foreign instrumentation signals intelligence
FLO	Foreign Liaison Office
FLOT	forward line of troops
FROG	free rocket over ground
FSU	former Soviet Union
FTX	field training exercise
FY	fiscal year

(continued)

Table 8.4. (*continued*)

Alphabetically by Abbreviation	
Abbreviation	*Full Name*
GCA	ground controlled approach
GCC	Gulf Cooperation Council; Government Control Center
GCI	ground controlled intercept
GDP	gross domestic product
GHq	general headquarters
GLCM	ground-launched cruise missile
GMT	Greenwich Mean Time
GNP	gross national product
GOB	ground order of battle
GRU	(Soviet) General Staff Intelligence Organization
HE	high explosive
HEAT	high-explosive antitank
HF	high frequency
HUMINT	human resources intelligence
ICBM	intercontinental ballistic missile
IDF	Israeli Defense Force
IFF	identification, friend or foe
I-HAWK	Improved-Homing-All-the-Way Killer
IIR	Intelligence Information Report; imaging infrared
IMF	International Monetary Fund
IMINT	imagery intelligence
INF	Intermediate-range Nuclear Force
IOC	initial operational capability
IR	infrared; Intelligence Information Report
IRBM	intermediate-range ballistic missile
I&W	indications and warning
JDA	Japan Defense Agency
JSDF	Japanese Self Defense Force
kg	kilogram; kilograms
KGB	Committee for State Security (Soviet)
km	kilometer; kilometers
km/h	kilometers/hour
kn	knot; knots
kt	kiloton; kilotons
kV	kilovolt; kilovolts
kW	kilowatt; kilowatts
LAF	Lebanese Armed Forces

Alphabetically by Abbreviation	
Abbreviation	Full Name
LASINT	laser intelligence
LF	low frequency
LOC(s)	line(s) of communication
LOX	liquid oxygen
LRA	Long-Range Aviation
MASINT	measurement and signature intelligence
MD	military district
MIRV	multiple independently-targetable reentry vehicle (warhead)
mm	millimeter; millimeters
MNF	Multinational Force
MOB	missile order of battle; main operating base
MR	military region
MRBM	medium-range ballistic missile
NAM	Nonaligned Movement
NATO	North Atlantic Treaty Organization
NCO	noncommissioned officer
NM	nautical mile(s)
NOB	naval order of battle
NSWP	Non-Soviet Warsaw Pact
NUCINT	nuclear intelligence
OAS	Organization of American States
OAU	Organization of African Unity
OB	order of battle
OECD	Organization for Economic Cooperation and Development
OPEC	Organization of Petroleum-Exporting Countries
OPINT	operational intelligence
OPSEC	operations security
OSINT	open-source intelligence
PBV	postboost vehicle
PHOTINT	photographic intelligence
PLO	Palestine Liberation Organization
POL	petroleum, oil, and lubricants
Polisario	Popular Front for the Liberation of Saguia el Hamra and Rio de Oro
POW, PW	prisoner of war
PRA	Permanent Restricted Area
RADINT	radar intelligence
R&D	research and development
ROB	radar order of battle

(continued)

Table 8.4. (*continued*)

Alphabetically by Abbreviation	
Abbreviation	Full Name
RO/RO	rollon/rolloff (ship)
RV	reentry vehicle
SADF	South African Defense Force
SALT	Strategic Arms Limitation Talks
SAM	surface-to-air missile
SDI	Strategic Defense Initiative
SIGINT	signals intelligence
SIGSEC	signals security
SLAR	side-looking airborne radar
SLBM	submarine (sea)-launched ballistic missile
SLCM	submarine-launched cruise missile
SP	self-propelled
SRBM	short-range ballistic missile
SRF	Strategic Rocket Forces (Soviet)
SSM	surface-to-surface missile
START	Strategic Arms Reduction Talks
S&TI	scientific and technical intelligence
STOL	short takeoff and landing
SWAPO	South-West Africa People's Organization
TASS	Official News Agency of the Former Soviet Union
Tel	transporter-erector-launcher
TELAR	transporter-erector-launcher and radar
TNF	Theater Nuclear Forces
TO&E	table of organization and equipment
TRA	Temporary Restricted Area
TVD	theater of military operations (Soviet)
UAV	unmanned aerial vehicle
UC	under construction
UHF	ultrahigh frequency
UI	unidentified
UK	United Kingdom
UN	United Nations
U.S.	United States
USSR	Union of Soviet Socialist Republics
VDV	Soviet airborne troops
VHF	very high frequency
VLF	very low frequency
V/STOL	vertical/short takeoff and landing

Alphabetically by Abbreviation	
Abbreviation	Full Name
VTA	Military Transport Aviation (Soviet)
VTOL	vertical takeoff and landing
WATCHCON	Watch Condition
WP	Warsaw Pact

be spelled out in full on first appearance, followed by the appropriate abbreviation in parentheses.

This table was compiled primarily for standardization purposes. It includes abbreviations, acronyms, and organizational designations. It is not intended to be comprehensive. The first section lists the abbreviations alphabetically by full name, and the second part lists them alphabetically by abbreviation as a ready reference guide.

For abbreviations not covered here, see the Joint Military Intelligence College publication *Defense and Intelligence Abbreviations and Acronyms* (Washington, DC: Defense Intelligence Agency, November 1997), edited by Dr. Russ Swenson. That publication, at this writing, is available online at <http://www.dia.mil/publicaffairs/Foia/abbrev_acron.pdf>.

Notes for Chapter 8

1. The former Soviet Union has split up; East and West Germany have united; so have North and South Yemen. Your papers, however, may include references in a historical sense to the former Soviet Union or the previously divided countries.

2. Navy enlisted personnel are identified by rate and rating (rate is the pay grade and rating is the specialty). The number of ratings is too numerous to list; however, the examples shown here are those of communications technicians.

3. Abbreviations are excerpted from the *U.S. GPO Style Manual* (2000 edition), 149.

9

Compound Words and Other Troublemakers

Demon Words and Phrases

Spelling, capitalization, hyphenation, and compounding of certain terms often vary from source to source. Table 9.1 contains some of the most common troublemakers and provides a quick, standardized reference. An excellent source for other problem words is the *U.S. Government Printing Office Style Manual*.[1]

The function of some words is indicated by the abbreviations adj. (adjective), n. (noun), or v. (verb). You will note that those words change form depending upon their part of speech—an odd quirk in the English language. For example, note the difference in the forms *hand out* and *handout* in the two sentences below:

> Branch chiefs are required to *hand out* their agendas before meetings begin. (verb)
> The *handout* for that meeting was helpful. (noun)

Note for Chapter 9

1. GPO *Style Manual* (2000), 75–124.

Table 9.1. List of Tourblemaking Words

able-bodied (adj.)	armor-heavy (adj.)	battleship
accommodate	armor officer	beachhead
ad hoc	armored brigade, unit	before-cited
adviser	army-group-level (adj.)	bellwether
Aeroflot	Atlantic Fleet	below-market (adj.)
airbase	back channel (n.)	benefited/-fiting
air-breathing	back-channel (v., adj.)	black market (n.)
aircrew	backdate	black-market (v., adj.)
airfield	back down (v.)	boatbuilder
air force (general use)	backdown (n., adj.)	boatcrew
airlift	backdrop	boatyard
airpower, but naval and air power	backfit	borderland
airspace	backspace	borderline
airstrike	backtrack	boresight
allied forces	backup (n., adj.)	born (birth)
allies (U.S. allies, but NATO Allies)	back up (v.)	borne (carried)
all-weather (adj.)	bailout (n., adj.)	bottleneck
antiaircraft	bail out (v.)	bottom line (n.)
antiballistic	balance-of-payments (adj.)	bottom-line (adj.)
anticommunist	ballistic missile (adj.)	brainstorm
antiguerrilla	base camp	brain trust
antimissile	baseline	brainwash
antinuclear	base line (surveying)	breakaway (n., adj.)
antisatellite	battalion-sized units	breakdown (n., adj.)
antitank	battlefront	break down (v.)
antiterrorist	battleground	break-in (n., adj.)
apparatus (sing.), apparatuses (pl.)	battle group	break in (v.)
Arafat, Yassir	battle line	breakout (n., adj.)

break out (v.)
breakthrough
break up (v.)
breakup (n., adj.)
breechloader
breech-loading (adj.)
bridgehead
building block (n.)
building-block (adj.)
buildingways (sing. and pl.)
buildup (n., adj.)
build up (v.)
built-in (adj.)
built-up (adj.)
burdensharing
canceled
cancellation
candlelit
cannot (one word, always)
carrier-based (adj.)
carrierborne
carryover (n., adj.)
carry over (v.)
catchup (adj.)
catch up (v.)
cease-fire (n., adj.)
cease fire (v.)
chain of command
chairman

chairperson
chairwoman
chief of staff
close-in (adj.)
closeminded
coal-mining (adj.)
coauthor
cochairman
codename (n.)
codenamed (adj., v.)
codeword
collocated
combatant
combat-capable (adj.)
command and control (n.)
command-and-control (adj.)
Commander in Chief (n.)
commandwide
communications chief, officer, or satellite
communism
communist
cost-effective (adj.)
counter-countermeasures
counterdrug
counterguerrilla
countermeasures
counternarcotics
counterproliferation

counterstrike
counterterrorist
countrywide
coworker
crack down (v.)
crackdown (n.)
craneway
cruise missile
cutback (n.)
CY 2009
cyberspace
database
decisionmaker, decisionmaking
de-escalate
de facto
defense attaché (but U.S. Defense Attaché)
disastrous
division-level (adj.)
double space
dry dock
dual-purpose (adj.)
dual-track (adj.)
early-to-mid-stage
Eastern Europe (n.), but East European (adj.)
electromagnetic
electro-optic
e-mail (hyphenated)

(continued)

Table 9.1. (*continued*)

embargoes	grant aid	in-country
embarrassment	grant-in-aid	in-depth (adj.)
en route	ground-based (adj.)	Intelink (capitalized, upper and lower case)
face-saving (adj.)	ground-controlled intercept	Intelligence Community
fallout	guided-missile destroyer	Internet (capitalized)
Far Eastern	half-loaded (adj.)	in-theater
farsighted	hand-carry	jetliner
feasible	hand grenade	joint task force
firepower	hand out (v.)	keyword
first hand	handout (n., adj.)	kickoff
five-year plan	harass	kidnapped
fixed-wing (adj.)	hardcore (adj.)	Khrushchev, Nikita
Fleet Marine Forces	hardline (adj.)	land-mobile (adj.)
flight test, but flight-testing	hardliner	large-scale (adj.)
follow-on (n., adj.)	hard-surface (adj.)	launch site
follow on (v.)	heavyhanded	launching ways
follow through (n., adj.)	height-finding (adj.)	leftwing (adj.)
followup (n., adj.)	helicopter-borne (adj.)	left wing (n.)
follow up (v.)	high-altitude (adj.)	liftoff
forums (not fora)	high frequency (n.)	lightweight
four-star (adj.)	high-frequency (adj.)	line-of-sight (adj.)
Free World	high-level (adj.)	liquid-propellant (adj.)
front-running	high-ranking (adj.)	live-fire (adj.)
full-time (adj.)	hindrance	long-range (adj.)
FY 2010	home base (n.), but home-based (v.)	longstanding
general purpose forces	home port (n.), but home-ported (v.)	long-term
glidepath (adj.)	hotbed	long-time (adj.)
government-in-exile (n.)	ill-timed (adj.)	

look angle (n.)
lookdown-shootdown (adj.)
loose-leaf
low-altitude (adj.)
lowercase (adj.)
low frequency (n.)
low-frequency (adj.)
low-level (adj.)
low-ranking (adj.)
Mach 2
machinegun
manmade (adj.)
man-portable (adj.)
martial-law (adj.)
mid-2009
midair
midday
Middle Eastern
mid-level
mid-range
midstage
mid-to-late stage
midyear
minefield
Modified SPRINT (Mod SPRINT)
multidiscipline
multipurpose
Muslim
narrowband

National Guard
national-level (adj.)
nationwide
NATO Alliance, NATO Allies
NATO forces
Near East
near-real-time (adj.)
near-term (adj.)
newfound
no-first-use policy
non-air-transportable
nonaligned (adj.)
noncommissioned
noncommunist
nondivisional
nonmilitary
nonnegotiable
nonnuclear
non-oil-producing
nonpartisan
non-Soviet Warsaw Pact
non-U.S. NATO forces
nose cone
nuclear-free zone
nuclear-weapons-free zone
number-one (adj.)
offline
offset
offshoot

offshore
often, *not* oftentimes or ofttimes
oil-producing (adj.)
onbase (adj.)
onboard (adj.)
ongoing
onhand (adj.)
online (adj.)
onsite (adj.)
onstation (adj.)
open-door (adj.)
Operations Other Than War (OOTW)
order of battle (n.)
order-of-battle (adj.)
outdated
outgoing
out-of-date (adj.)
overhaul
overriding
paramilitary
part-time (adj.)
peacekeeping
phasedown (n., adj.)
phase-in (n., adj.)
phase in (v.)
phaseout (n., adj.)
phase out (v.)
photographic
photoreconnaissance

(continued)

Table 9.1. (*continued*)

play down (v.)	reentry	slow down (v.)
policymaker, policymaking	reevaluate	so-called (adj.)
pontoon	Regular Army	solid-propellant (adj.)
postattack	repairway	South Atlantic
postboost	reverse-engineer (v.)	South Pacific
post-Cold War	rightwing (adj.)	Southeast Asia
postwar	right wing (n.)	Southern Atlantic
powerplant	rollback (n.)	Southwest Pacific
preattack	roll back (v.)	space age (n.)
precision-guided (adj.)	rotary-wing (adj.)	space-age (adj.)
preexamine	safe house (n.)	space-based (adj.)
pre-position	sealift	spaceborne
programmed	second-generation (adj.)	space flight
pullout (n.)	second-largest (adj.)	space station
pull out (v.)	seize	splashdown
Qadhafi, Muammar	servicemember	staging area
quandary	servicemen, servicewomen	standdown (n.)
quasi- (adj.)	setback (n.)	stand down (v.)
quick-reaction	set back (v.)	standing operating procedures
radio broadcast	shakeup (n.)	standoff
radio-relay (adj.)	shake up (v.)	state of the art (n.)
radio set	sheikh	state-of-the-art (adj.)
railyard	shore-based (adj.)	steel-producing
rapprochement	short-range (adj.)	Strategic Arms Limitation Talks
Ready Reserve	siege	streamlined
real-time (adj.)	silo-based (adj.)	strongman (nonliteral)
re-engineer	slowdown (n.)	Sub-Saharan Africa (n.)

Sub-Saharan African (adj.)
subsystem
super high frequency (n.)
super-high-frequency (adj.)
superpowers
surface-to-air missile
swingwing
takeoff (n.)
take off (v.)
takeover (n.)
take over (v.)
targeted, targeteer, targeting
telecommunications
test-fire (v.)
third country (n.)
third-country (adj.)
third party (n.)
third-party (adj.)
Third World (n.)
Third-World (adj.)
threshold
throw-weight (adj.)
trade-in (n., adj.)
trade in (v.)
tradeoff (n., adj.)

trade off (v.)
transporter-erector-launcher
transporter-erector-launcher-and-radar
transshipment
traveled, traveler, traveling
triservice
trooplift
T-shaped (adj.)
turnout (n.)
turn out (v.)
ultrahigh frequency (n.)
ultrahigh-frequency (adj.)
underway
update, updated (n., v., adj.)
uppercase (adj.)
U.S.-leased (adj.)
U.S.-made (adj.)
U.S. military forces
very-high frequency (n.)
very-high-frequency (adj.)
very-low frequency (n.)
very-low-frequency (adj.)
warfighter, warfighting (one word)
war game (n.)
war-game (v., adj.)

wargaming
Warsaw Pact forces
weapon systems
website
Western (nations)
Western Alliance
Western Atlantic
Western Europe (n.), but West
    European (adj.)
westernmost
Western Pacific
white paper (diplomatic)
wideband
wide-ranging (adj.)
workday
working-class (adj.)
working-level (adj.)
worldwide, but World Wide Web
    (WWW)
xenophobia
yearend
yearlong
year-old
zero-option (adj.)
ZULU time

10

A Usage Glossary for Intelligence Writers

a/an Use *an* before words that begin with a vowel *sound* (an apple, an heir). "An historian" is incorrect because the *h* is sounded; but, "*an* hour." "An unique idea" is incorrect also, because the initial sound in *unique* is that of the consonant *y*; but, "*an* unwarranted assumption."

abbreviations and acronyms Shortened forms of words and phrases can be useful at times, such as in a newspaper ad where you pay by the word or line. Avoid the use of non-standard abbreviations or acronyms wherever possible. When you do use one, spell it out the first time, then put the short form in parentheses; thereafter you may use the short form: for example, Strategic Defense Initiative (SDI).

adapt/adopt *To adapt* is to adjust oneself to a new or changed situation. *To adopt* is to choose and follow a new course of action: "East German leaders found it difficult to *adapt* to the wave of democracy sweeping Eastern Europe. The people, however, readily *adopted* democracy."

advance/advanced *Advance* party; *advance* payment; *advanced* training program.

adverse/averse Both words are adjectives. Most nations had an *adverse* (unfavorable) reaction to North Korea's handling of its nuclear program. The United Nations, however, was *averse* (disinclined) to imposing sanctions.

advice/advise *Advice*, a noun, is counsel or assistance that is given. *Advise* is a verb. "The lieutenant could not *advise* me what to do, so I took the sergeant's *advice*."

affect/effect Both words may be verbs. To *affect* something is to have an impression on it or to change it: "Glasnost may *affect* our foreign policy." To *effect* something is to create it: "The Soviets *effected* a change in their policy with glasnost." Effect may also be a noun, meaning result or consequence: "The *effects* of glasnost remain to be seen."

afterward/afterwards *Afterward* is preferred.

all/all of Except when a personal pronoun is involved ("We saw all of them."), "of" is redundant. "They interviewed *all* the candidates."

all ready/already *All ready* means everyone or everything is ready: "The troops were *all ready* for muster." *Already* means before a specified or implied time: "Private Jones was missing, and it was *already* time for muster."

all right/alright *All right* is the correct form; *alright* is not a word.

all together/altogether *All together* means in unison: "The analysts were *all together* in their assessment." *Altogether* means all told, in all, or completely: "The analysts were *altogether* confused about the new developments."

allude/elude/illusion *To allude* to something is to mention it indirectly. The noun form is *allusion*. "Her *allusion* to the bastions of communism made me think of Cuba and North Korea." One gets away or escapes by *eluding*. "He *eluded* capture for 15 days before being rescued." Finally, an *illusion* is something that is not really there—a mistaken impression or belief. "Absolute certainty in intelligence estimates is an *illusion*."

along with *Along with* does not affect the verb: "The captain, *along with* other personnel, was on deck." This rule also holds true for *as well as, in addition to, like,* and *together with.*

alot/a lot *Alot* is not a word. There is a word *allot*, meaning "to distribute, or to assign shares or portions," but that is usually not what the writer of "alot" has in mind. Most of the time a better sentence will result by rewriting to avoid the use of "a lot"; even though grammatically correct, it is imprecise.

Incorrect: *Alot* of reservists are leaving the service early.
Correct: *A lot* of reservists are leaving the service early.
Better: Almost 60 percent of reservists are leaving the service early.

altar/alter   You are likely to find an *altar* in a place of worship, where one's attitude might be *altered* (changed).

alternate/alternative   Used as a verb, a noun, or an adjective (and pronounced differently depending upon its usage), *alternate* means to change back and forth in turn or to substitute. "They *alternate* their shift work, producing *alternate* estimates in the process." *Alternatives* are choices: "They had no *alternative* but to accept the figures given in the assessment." It is redundant to use the word "other" with alternatives; that is, do not write "We had no *other* alternative."

altitude/elevation   Use *altitude* when describing something in the air, *elevation* when referring to the ground: "The new jet fighter may attain a record *altitude*." "The *elevation* of that mountain range averages 7,000 meters."

amid/amidst   *Amidst* sounds poetic, but it is not for intelligence writing. Use *amid*.

among/amongst   You will be right at home in the United Kingdom with *amongst*, but as long as you're writing papers in the United States, the preferred form is *among*.

among/between   *Among* always implies more than two: "War reparations were distributed among the six nations." *Between* expresses the relationship of two things: "There was a dispute *between* the two countries." But *between* is also used for more than two to indicate a reciprocal relationship: "A treaty was concluded *between* the three nations."

amount/number   *Amount* refers to things judged by their weight, bulk, or sums: "The *amount* of cargo carried by the new truck is impressive." *Number* refers to things that can be counted: "The rebels lost a staggering *number* of men in August." See also "fewer/less."

analyzation   This is an ostentatious way of saying *analysis*.

and/or   Means one or the other or both. Obviously imprecise. Avoid this form.

anymore   Always spell this as two words: *any more*.

appraise/apprise   *Appraise* means to assign a value to something. "We were unable to *appraise* the worth of the captured equipment." *Apprise* means to tell. "Our commander *apprised* us of the situation."

approximately/about/some   Never use these words when a figure is stated precisely.

> Incorrect: We counted approximately 37 tanks. Some 64 divisions opposed us.
>
> Correct: We counted approximately 40 tanks and more than 60 divisions facing us.

> (*Note:* All estimates should be rounded. Also, do not use the words "estimated" and "approximately" [about, some] together, because they both show approximations.)

assure/ensure/insure   All mean to make sure or certain. *Assure* applies to persons. It alone has the sense of setting a person's mind at rest: "I *assured* the professor of my attentiveness." *Ensure* implies making an outcome certain or making something safe: "Abundant crops *ensure* a nation against famine." *Insure* means to cover with insurance. The distinction between *ensure* and *insure* is disappearing in American English usage. While it is in transition, though, you should distinguish between the two in your formal writing. Consult a current dictionary if you have any doubt about correct usage.

as well as   See "along with."

at present/currently/presently   These terms are overused in intelligence writing: "The situation is stable *at present*." "They *currently* have shortages of men and materiel." In almost every case the term may be omitted because the present tense of the verb—"is," "have"—already conveys that meaning.

average   An *average* can be only one figure.

> Incorrect: The new Fizzle fighter *averages* between 900 and 1,000 knots.
>
> Correct: The new Fizzle fighter *averages* 950 knots.

averse   See "adverse/averse."

awhile/a while   *Awhile* is an adverb, analogous to expressions such as *ago*, in "a month *ago*." Use *awhile* in constructions such as "We rested *awhile*." With a preposition, use the noun form "(a) while," as in "We rested for *a while*."

because of   See "due to."

between/among   See "among/between."

boat/ship   A *ship* is a large vessel, capable of going to sea. A *boat* is relatively small, stays mostly in coastal or inland waters, and can be carried on a ship.

can/may   The attentive writer will use *can* for ability or power to do something, and *may* for permission to do it: "Even though our children *can* write on the walls, it is unlikely that we will say they *may* do so." *Note*: In intelligence writing, "can" is often used as a synonym for "has the capability to" or "is capable of," when speaking of a nation or force's capabilities: "The North Koreans *can* exercise that option at any time." The word does not, and should not, imply any *intention*. "May," on the other hand, is used to imply a probability: "The Cubans *may* be serious about improving trade relations." To facilitate understanding, substitute "might" in the previous sentence.

capital/capitol   The *capital* is the city or the money, or an adjective meaning first or primary (capital letter, capital offense, capital punishment); the *capitol* is a building. To remember, think of the round, O-like dome of the capitOl building.

careen/career   Although these two words are often used interchangeably, they have different meanings. To *careen* is to sway from side to side: "Our ship *careened* dangerously in the heavy seas." As a noun, *career* means a profession; but as a verb it means to go at top speed, especially in a headlong or reckless manner: "The tank *careered* out of control down the hill."

center around/center about   Neither of these phrases is correct. Use *center upon* or *center on*. "U.S. foreign policy is said to *center upon* neo-Wilsonian pragmatism."

cite/site/sight   *Cite* is a verb, meaning to quote, mention, or commend: "She *cited* the dictionary as her source." "The captain *cited* the sergeant for bravery." *Site*, as a noun, means a place: "We visited the *site* of the battle." Used as a verb, it means to locate something on a site: "They *sited* the new classroom building in Columbia, Maryland." *Sight* may be either a verb or a noun, and means the act or fact of seeing: "She *sighted* the classroom building. His *sight* was inadequate at night."

collocate To set or place together. *Not* spelled "colocate," although some dictionaries now differ.

communication/communications Both words may be either a noun or an adjective. *Communication* refers to the process or the act of communicating: "Skills in interpersonal *communication* are essential for intelligence professionals." *Communications* are the means of sending messages: "The *communications* satellite provides instantaneous transmission worldwide."

compare to/with To compare one thing *to* another is to emphasize the similarity between the two: "She *compared* the Soviet tank regiment *to* a U.S. Army armored battalion." To compare one thing *with* another is to examine all aspects and qualities for similarity or dissimilarity, as in "He *compared* the regiment *with* the division."

complement/compliment A ship's crew is its *complement*; one object or event may complete or coordinate with another. A positive comment about another person is a *compliment*. "The professor *complimented* Jones on his writing."

compose/comprise/constitute These three words are often confused. *Comprise* means to embrace, include, or contain—the whole *comprises* the parts. Conversely, the parts *constitute* or *compose* the whole. "The home guard *comprises* ten units." "Ten units *constitute* (or compose) the home guard."

compounding words Compounding confounds many students. Some of the most common compound words you will encounter are in the following list. Notice how they are formed:

anticommunist, antiguerrilla, antiterrorist; *but*, anti-American, anti-European counterguerrilla, counterterrorism, counterterrorist

conduct A vague, overused word, as in "The Iranians *conducted* an amphibious operation." Instead, try *engaged in*, *launched*, or *performed*.

continual/continuous *Continual* means frequently repeated with only brief interruptions: "*Continual* misunderstandings highlighted the negotiations." *Continuous* means absolutely without interruption: "*Continuous* misunderstandings marred the seventh day of negotiations."

contractions Do not use them in formal writing.

council/counsel *Counsel* is both a noun and a verb. You might need to secure legal *counsel* if you want to breach a contract agreement. Your lawyer will *counsel* you then on your rights. A *council* is some form of advisory committee. Perhaps you will argue that the ruling *council* needs to word its contract more clearly.

courts-martial/court-martials Either is acceptable, but *courts-martial* is preferred as the plural form.

crisis Denotes a turning point, a period of abrupt and decisive change. Iraq's invasion of Kuwait was a *crisis*; frequent changes of government in an unstable political environment are not. The plural form is *crises*.

criteria/criterion A *criterion* is a standard for judgment; the plural form is *criteria*: "One *criterion* of a well-written paper is clarity, but many other *criteria* also contribute to readability."

currently See "at present/currently/presently."

data/errata/media/phenomena These are the plural forms of *datum* (rarely used), *erratum*, *medium*, and *phenomenon*, respectively. Each requires a plural verb.

dates/decades Use commas after the day and the year when you write a complete date (month, day, year) within a sentence. "Her assessment is given in the March 11, 2008, estimate." Style and grammar guides differ on this one, however; so consult yours for guidance.

deactivate/inactivate Both words mean to make inactive. In military usage, *deactivate* usually means rendering explosives inert. *Inactivate* is to disband or cause to go out of existence a military unit, government agency, or other organized body.

different from/than *Different from* is the preferred term. (Even better, *differs from*.) "This rule is *different from* that one." However, if the object of the preposition is a clause, *different than* is preferred: "How *different* things appear in Washington *than* in Paris."

dilemma A *dilemma* is a situation involving distasteful alternatives. Avoid using the term when all you are discussing is a problem. Preferred synonyms include *plight*, *predicament*, or *quandary*. Avoid the trite "horns of a dilemma."

disburse/disperse To *disburse* is to pay out or distribute: "The pay officer *disbursed* the monthly payroll to the troops." To *disperse* is to scatter or spread something: "National Guard troops *dispersed* the crowd."

discreet/discrete *Discreet* means showing good judgment or being able to maintain a prudent silence: "An intelligence professional must always be *discreet* in handling classified information." *Discrete* means separate, distinct: "The intelligence process has three *discrete* phases: collection, production, and dissemination."

disinterested/uninterested *Disinterested* means impartial, unbiased: "You should have your first written draft read by a *disinterested* individual." A mediator should be *disinterested*. *Uninterested* means indifferent: "The students appeared *uninterested* in my topic for discussion."

dissent/dissension *Dissent* can be both a noun and a verb. If you do not agree with a particular policy, you can *dissent* or "differ in opinion." Such a difference of opinion is called a *dissent* or a *dissenting* opinion. *Dissension* (note the spelling) goes beyond a difference of opinion—which can be expressed amicably—and indicates discord or quarreling.

due to/because of/owing to/on account of Grammar textbooks and dictionaries disagree on proper usage for this term, but in most cases of standard written English, *due to* is becoming acceptable as a prepositional phrase. Technically, though, *due* is an adjective that needs a noun to modify. If *due to* comes after a form of the verb *to be*, then *due* is being used—correctly—as an adjective: "The project's failure was *due to* insufficient planning." (The adjective *due* modifies the noun *failure*.) *Because of*, *owing to*, and *on account of* are compound prepositions: "The project failed *because of* (or owing to, on account of) insufficient planning." Avoid beginning a sentence with *due to*.

Incorrect: *Due to* improper assembly, the temporary bridge collapsed.

Correct: *Because of* improper assembly, the temporary bridge collapsed.

Also correct: The collapse of the temporary bridge was *due* to improper assembly.

each *Each*, used as a subject, takes a singular verb and related pronoun: "*Each* student, graduate and undergraduate, *has* his or her own style of writing."

each and every Redundant. *Each* is enough by itself.

east/eastern Indefinite or general terms of broad application commonly end in *-ern* and are not capitalized unless they refer to specific blocs (see the next entry): "The unit trained in the *eastern* part of the country." Terms of definite designation commonly use the short form, as in "the *east* bank of the river" or "the *east* side of town."

East/Soviet bloc These terms are vague and may confuse your reader. Be precise in writing about former communist countries or regional alliances. The term "Eastern Europe," for example, includes the former non-Soviet Warsaw Pact countries, the former Yugoslavia, and Albania.

economic/economics/economical *Economic*, an adjective, pertains to the science of economics, a singular noun: "The country devalued its currency because of *economic* problems." "*Economics* is an imprecise science." *Economical* means thrifty: "Cutting $50 from my food budget was an *economical* move."

effect See "affect/effect."

e.g. *E.g.* is the abbreviation for *exempli gratia*, meaning "for example." Do not confuse it with *i.e.* (*id est*), which means "that is." They are *not* interchangeable. It is best just to avoid the abbreviations and spell out "for example" or "that is."

either . . . or/neither . . . nor   When all elements of an *either. . . or/neither . . . nor* construction are singular or plural, the verb is singular or plural, respectively: "*Either* DIA *or* CIA *has* the information I need." "*Neither* the studies from DIA *nor* the estimates from CIA *have* the data I am seeking." When the elements differ, the verb takes the number of the nearer element: "*Either* the heavy rain *or* the elephants *are* responsible for the ground-cover loss."

electronic/electronics   The singular form is an adjective: "The Special Operations Forces have sophisticated *electronic* equipment." The plural form is a noun and takes a singular verb when it refers to the science as a whole: "*Electronics is* a complicated science." Often, in intelligence writing, the term takes a plural verb: "The *electronics* of that new aircraft *are* incredibly complex." *Note:* The term "*electronics*" is usually used in place of a phrase such as "the electronic components" or "the suite of electronics."

elevation   See "altitude/elevation."

elicit/illicit   You *elicit* information, a confession, or a response of some kind by coaxing or bringing forth; the word is a verb: "The interrogator skillfully *elicited* a response from the refugee." The adjective *illicit* means illegal, unlawful: "The Department of Defense is working closely with the Drug Enforcement Administration to curb *illicit* drug trafficking."

emigrate/immigrate   People emigrate *from* a country and immigrate *to* a country. Remember: "*em-*" = "*exit*," and "*im-*" = "*into*."

eminent/imminent   An *eminent* person is famous or otherwise well known in his or her field: "The faculty recognized Dr. Rongar as the *eminent* authority in intelligence analysis." *Imminent* means "about to happen," as in the *imminence* of hostilities.

enormity   Many frown on using *enormity* to indicate bigness. Use it instead to refer to "monstrous wickedness." "The enormity of Saddam Hussein's treatment of Kurds created unrest in Iraq for decades." Do not write about the *enormity* of the coalition's decision to liberate Kuwait—unless you are a member of the Iraqi army.

ensure   See "assure/ensure/insure."

errata   See "data/errata/media/phenomena."

et al.   The Latin abbreviation for *et alii* or *et alia*, meaning "and others." Why not just say "and others"?

etc./et cetera   Another of those perfectly good Latin phrases, meaning "and so forth"; but do not use it in intelligence writing, because it signals your readers that you are leaving it up to them to complete whatever list you ended with that phrase: "The new battlefield formation is known to have tanks, armored personnel carriers, air defense artillery, *etc.*" (Might the "etc." include chemical weapons?)

eventhough   Not a word. Use *even though*.

everyday/every day   *Everyday* means ordinary: "Military maneuvers are an *everyday* occurrence in that training area." *Every day* means daily: "We observe their training *every day*."

everyone/everybody   As subjects, these words take singular verbs: "*Everyone (or Everybody) is* expected to agree on the latest intelligence assessment."

explicit   Sometimes confused with its opposite, *implicit*. An *explicit* understanding has been stated: "The United Nations warning to North Korea was *explicit*." An *implicit* understanding is perceived, but has not been expressly stated: "The diplomats adjourned their session with an *implicit* understanding of the terms of reference."

explosive/explosives   Use *explosive* in specific reference to a bursting or propelling charge (high explosive). Normally the plural form is used in such expressions as "*explosives* storage."

(the) fact that   The phrase "*the fact that*" can usually be avoided with a little rewriting. The phrase "due to the fact that" can *always* be replaced by "because."

fake analysis   Avoid "phony" phrases such as the following: anything can happen; further developments are expected; it is difficult to determine; it is not possible to predict; it is too early to tell; it remains to be seen; only the future will tell; only time will tell.

farther/further   *Farther* is generally applied to physical distance: "It is *farther* from Moscow to Vladivostok than it is from Chicago to Honolulu." *Further* is used for a metaphorical distance: "His assessment could not be *further* from the truth."

fear   Fear is an extreme emotion. The word should not be applied to ordinary concern or uneasiness.

> Incorrect: "We *fear* that the armed forces are having another reorganization."
>
> Correct: Use "we believe" or "we estimate" instead.

feel   *Feel* as a synonym for *believe* or *think* is sloppy usage.

fewer/less   *Fewer* refers to numbers or units considered individually: "We have *fewer* order of battle analysts than the other section." *Less* refers to quantity or degree: "We published *less* material this month because of the shortage of analysts."

flounder/founder   When a ship fills with water and sinks, it *founders*. When a horse breaks down, it also *founders*. So too if an enterprise or plan totally collapses, it may be said to *founder*. Hope still remains if the verb is *flounder*, which means to struggle helplessly in embarrassment or confusion.

forego/forgo   For *precede*, use *forego*: "The key judgment of that estimate appeared to be a *foregone* conclusion." For *relinquish*, use *forgo*: "I must *forgo* attending the conference because of a shortage of travel funds."
(*Note:* Often sentences with *forgo*, like the previous one, can be rewritten more forcefully: "I cannot attend the conference because of a shortage of travel funds.")

foreseeable future/near term   Fuzzy clichés. Your "foreseeable future" might be someone else's "near term." Be specific.

former   See "latter/last/first/former."

forthcoming   Means about to appear, or available when required or as promised: "The *forthcoming* estimate will address that issue." Avoid the usage intended to mean cooperative or outgoing, because of the possibility of confusion: "The Ambassador was *forthcoming*."

from . . . to   The sentence, "The exercise took place *from* 1 *to* 5 October" means that it was a 4-day exercise, *not including* the final date. To include the final date, the phrase should read "from 1 *through* 5 October."

gender See "he or she."

he or she vs. he/she or s/he The commotion about gender-specific nouns and pronouns is not likely to go away soon. The use of *he or she* (*him or her* and *his or her*) is one solution, but many writers find it cumbersome. The slashed constructions *he/she* and *s/he* are ugly. The least annoying option is to use plurals. Instead of writing "A student should carefully research his topic," write "Students should carefully research their topics." Note that *service members*, not just *servicemen*, died in the Iraq war.

headquarters May take either a singular or a plural verb. "His *headquarters is* in Washington" implies only one building or organization. "Their *headquarters are* in Washington" means more than one building or organization.

historic/historical *Historic* means important in the framework of history: "Gettysburg was a *historic* battle." *Historical* can mean the same thing, but also covers other things concerned with history: "*The Killer Angels* is a *historical* novel."

hopefully Some diehard grammatical conservatives will argue with you over this one, but modern English language usage is accepting *hopefully* in the sense of "it is hoped" or "I hope." Note the following usage citation from the Random House *Unabridged Dictionary*:

> Although some strongly object to its use as a sentence modifier, *hopefully* meaning "it is hoped (that)" has been in use since the 1930s and is fully standard in all varieties of speech and writing: *Hopefully, tensions between the two nations will ease.* This use of *hopefully* is parallel to that of *certainly, curiously, frankly, regrettably*, and other sentence modifiers.[1]

Hopefully, that will clarify the issue. Nonetheless, you should use the term sparingly in writing with intelligence, especially when you are writing estimative intelligence. Remember that you are expressing a personal hope or desire for something to happen when you say *hopefully*. That may not be your intent; for example: "*Hopefully,* the government of Panaragua will solve its problems in the long term."

however, comma   The word *however* seems to cause more problems for students than any other single word in the English language. Remember that *however* almost always requires punctuation on both sides of it. When a complete sentence (an independent clause) is on both sides of it, precede it with a period or semicolon and follow it with a comma: "I proofread my paper 13 times; *however,* the professor still found errors." If it has no complete sentence before it or after it, *however,* the word may be set off by commas on both sides. Notice that the phrase preceding "however" in the previous sentence and after it in the following sentence is not a complete sentence: "My paper was perfect, *however,* when I handed it in the 14th time."

hyphens   A few of the common uses of hyphens in your papers will be as unit modifiers and as substitutes for a printed dash. *Unit modifiers* are combinations of words that stand before a noun as a single unit, modifying it as a whole rather than in part. For example, you might write: "No change is expected in the short term." But, written another way, *short term* becomes a unit modifier: "The short-term outlook is bleak." Apply the same principle to such phrases as *long-term and high-level.* In the printing process, a dash is used in certain grammatical constructions. When the occasion calls for it, use two hyphens—typed together with no space between them on either side—as we have used them in this sentence. Microsoft Word automatically converts those two hyphens to an em dash.

i.e.   See "*e.g.*"

illicit   See "elicit/illicit."

illusion   See "allude/elude."

immigrate   See "emigrate/immigrate."

imminent   See "eminent/imminent."

impending/pending   *Pending* means yet to come or awaiting settlement: "Our assessment of the situation is *pending* coordination." *Impending* adds a hint of threat or menace: "*Impending* economic sanctions promise to cause severe problems for the military dictatorship."

implicit   See "explicit/implicit."

imply/infer   The writer or speaker *implies* when stating something indirectly: "She *implied* in her article that there might be a coup d'état." Readers or listeners *infer* when drawing a conclusion or making a deduction based upon what they have read or heard: "I *inferred* a mistaken conclusion from his estimate."

important/importantly   When introducing a second and more worthy consideration, *more important* is preferable to *more importantly*: "The truth is evident; *more important*, it will prevail."

in/into   *In* indicates location or condition; *into* suggests movement, direction, or change of condition.

inactivate   See "deactivate/inactivate."

in addition to   See "along with."

incite/insight   *Incite*, a verb, means to stir up or cause to happen, often with violence suggested: "The Homeland Guard troops *incited* a riot in front of the U.S. Embassy." The noun *insight* means an act of comprehension or understanding, especially through intuition. "Her *insight* into the Iraqi culture was unique."

(to) include   Used by bureaucrats to mean *including*: "The rebels received 12 tons of arms, *to include* 130 grenade launchers." Use *including*. There is a place for "to include," as in the following: "They updated their estimate *to include* [for the purpose of including] the latest information."

incomparables   Terms such as *very unique, more fatal,* and *more equal* are misuses of words that express absolutes. That which is unique, fatal, or equal can be no more or less so. Other incomparable words include *absolute, eternal, final, perfect, supreme, total,* and *unanimous.*

infer   See "imply/infer."

infrastructure   Bureaucratically ostentatious. Try *foundation* or *framework* instead.

in regards to   Use *in regard to* or, better yet, *regarding*: "We have not heard from her *regarding* the changes to our publication."

inside/outside (of)   When *inside* is used as a preposition, the "of" is unnecessary: "*Inside* the house" and "*inside* the circle of terrorists" are acceptable usages. The same principle is true of *outside* and *all*.

insight   See "incite/insight."

insure   See "assure/ensure/insure."

interface   An overused term, best avoided.

irregardless   There is no such word. Use either *regardless* or *irrespective*.

it is   Avoid this pair of words, especially at the beginning of a sentence or phrase. The result will usually be better prose.

> Not: "It is necessary that the L-14 fastener be redesigned."
> But: "The L-14 fastener must be redesigned."
> Even better (using active voice): "Widgits Inc. must redesign the L-14 fastener."

its/it's   *It's* always means "it is" or "it has." The possessive form of the pronoun *it* is *its*. You would not say *their's* or *your's*, so do not misuse the possessive form here.
(*Note:* It is best simply to avoid contractions in formal writing. If you do not use them in your papers, then you will never misuse *it's*.)

judgment   The preferred spelling is the one at left, *not* the chiefly British "judgement."

last/latest   *Last* denotes finality, while *latest* can mean only the most recent: "This is the *latest* of Captain Szwerdlodvski's reports; because he was shot just after he mailed it, it is also his *last*."

latter/last/first/former   *Latter* is applied only to the second of two items. A writer referring to the final one of three or more items would use *last*: "To assist you, I am sending Lieutenant Smith and Ensign Bowen, the *latter* because of his experience in riverine warfare." Similarly, *former* is applied only to the first of two items. If more than two items are listed, use the terms *first* and *last*.

lead/led   *Led* is the past tense of the verb form *to lead*: "The captain *led* his men bravely." *Lead*, when pronounced "led," is the metal.

less   See "fewer/less."

like   Also see "along with." The word *like* is never a conjunction and should not be used to replace *as*, *as if*, or *as though*. If you can substitute the words "similar to" or "similarly to," and the sentence still makes sense, then the word you want is *like*.

> Incorrect: "The new regime deals with insurgencies like the old dictatorship dealt with them."
>
> Correct: "The new regime deals with insurgencies as the old dictatorship dealt with them."
>
> Also correct: "The new regime deals with insurgencies similar to the old dictatorship."

like/such as   *Like* introduces a comparison with something else: "Hills in this part of the country are low and rounded *like* those near the coast." *Such as* introduces an example of the group itself: "Special operations forces *such as* Army Rangers and Navy SEALs are elite units."

likely   When *likely* is used as an adverb, it must be preceded by such qualifiers as *very*, *quite*, or *most*. Otherwise, it is incorrect, as in: "The Pakistani forces *likely* will deploy their tanks." *Likely*, as an adjective expressing inclination or probability, is followed by the infinitive: "The armed forces are *likely* to have a difficult time restoring order."

locate(d)   The term *locate(d)* is overused in intelligence writing, as in "The installation is *located* 60 km west of here." Often the term can be eliminated with no harm done: "The installation is 60 km west of here."

logistic/logistics/logistical   *Logistic* as the adjective and *logistics* as the noun form are preferred. *Logistical* is discouraged.

loose/lose   The error with this pair of words tends to be one of careless spelling rather than improper usage. Remember that *loose* rhymes with *goose* and *lose* rhymes with *choose*. "He could *lose* his job as security chief if the guard dogs get *loose*."

material/materiel   In military usage, *materiel* means arms, ammunition, and equipment.

may   See "can/may."

media   A plural form. See "data/errata/media/phenomena."

methodology If *method* or *system* is meant, use those words and avoid the term *methodology* (the study of the science of methods).

militate/mitigate *Militate* means to have weight or effect, for or against: "The facts *militate* against his interpretation." *Mitigate* means to appease, lessen, moderate, or soften: "*Mitigating* circumstances affected her assessment."

moral/morale *Moral* is an adjective meaning "having to do with right conduct." *Morale* is a noun meaning "degree of cheerfulness and confidence." Confusing the two can be comical: "The opposing forces had low *moral*."

more than one Takes a singular verb: "More than one division *was* involved in the exercise."

multiple qualifiers Avoid using more than one qualifier to describe a situation, such as "suggests . . . may," "may possibly," "could perhaps," "probably indicates," "reportedly may," and "suggests the possibility that the Army might deploy its forces."

munition/munitions The -s form is generally used: munitions storage building, munitions loading area.

myself This word is a reflexive pronoun, often erroneously used where *I* or *me* would be correct.

Incorrect:	Ambassador Myslinski and myself agree that the plan should go forward.
Correct:	Ambassador Myslinski and I . . . .
Incorrect:	Any such orders must be approved by Ambassador Catlin or myself.
Correct:	. . . Catlin or me.)

near term Fuzzy. See "foreseeable future/near term."

neither . . . nor See "either . . . or."

Non-Soviet Warsaw Pact A specific term for the six nations of the former Warsaw Treaty Organization ("Warsaw Pact"): Bulgaria, Czechoslovakia, the German Democratic Republic (East Germany), Hungary, Poland, and Romania.

none/not one Depending on what you intend, *none* may be singular or plural. When the meaning is *not one* or *no one*, the verb is singular: "*None* of the treaties *was* ratified by the newly elected president." Sometimes, though, the meaning of the sentence is clearly plural; in these cases, *none* takes a plural verb: "*None are* so ambitious as those who desire absolute power." (In the latter case, you might also have said: "*None is* so ambitious as one who desires absolute power.")

north/northern See "east/eastern." The same principles apply.

not only/but also These terms are called correlative conjunctions, and as such they must be followed by grammatically similar words or phrases. If *not only* is followed by a verb, then for the sake of parallelism, *but also* must have a verb after it as well. For example: "The student *not only* wrote his thesis during the summer *but also* took a vacation."

number/amount See "amount/number."

number, the/a When *number* is preceded by *the*, a *singular* verb is required: "*The number* of well-written theses *has* increased dramatically this year." If *number* is preceded by *a*, the verb is plural: "*A number* of students *have* failed this year because they could not write well."

numbers/numerals Keep a few rules in mind when you use numbers: Spell out one through nine; use numerals for 10 or more: "We saw one smoker and nine nonsmokers in the designated smoking area during the break." However, if the numbers are mixed—some below nine and some above—use all numerals: "A total of 3 smokers and 472 nonsmokers used the facilities today." Always spell out a number at the beginning of a sentence, unless it becomes unwieldy; then rewrite the sentence: "Twelve thousand men died in that battle." But: "Total losses were 11,991." Not: "Eleven thousand nine hundred ninety-one men died."

offload/unload *Unload* is preferred.

ongoing Try *continuing*, *underway*, or *in progress*, or leave it out altogether and see if your sentence still makes sense: "The *ongoing* research will prove my hypothesis." Better: "Research will prove my hypothesis."

only Place *only* as close as possible to the word it modifies, to avoid ambiguity. Observe the change in meaning caused by shifting *only* in the following sentences: "*Only* I wrote the correct answer for the professor." (No one else did.) "I *only* wrote the correct answer for the professor." (I did nothing else.) "I wrote *only* the correct answer for the professor." (I wrote nothing else.) "I wrote the *only* correct answer for the professor." (No other answers were correct.) "I wrote the correct answer *only* for the professor." (Or, for the professor *only*.) (And nothing else; or, I wrote it for no one else. This one is ambiguous.) Other words requiring similar treatment include *almost*, *even*, *merely*, and *scarcely*.

operation/operations   Use the singular as a modifier: *operation* map, *operation* plan, *operation* order (in each case, presumably one specific operation pertains). But acceptable usages include *operations* center, *operations* building, *operations* research, and *operations* officer.

optimize   A word to be avoided, like many other words that end in "*-ize*."

oral/verbal   Spoken words are *oral*. Anything constructed of words, either spoken or written, is *verbal*.

outside/inside (of)   See "inside/outside (of)."

overall   As an adjective, *overall* is much overworked and vague. Consider substitutes such as *average, complete, comprehensive, total*, or *whole*.

parameter   A word often overused in bureaucratic prose to mean boundary, limit, or outline.

parliamentarian   The word means an expert on parliamentary procedure. It does *not* mean "a member of Parliament."

partially/partly   These words are not interchangeable. *Partially* carries the sense of "to a certain degree"; it means "incompletely," as in "*partially* dependent." *Partly* stresses the part in contrast to the whole; it is equivalent to "in part."

pending/impending   See "impending/pending."

percentages   Spell out the percentage (10 percent); do not use the % sign. Always use numerals: 1 percent; 100 percent.

phenomena   A plural form. See "data/errata/media/phenomena."

phony phrases   See "fake analysis."

practicable/practical   *Practicable* means that which appears achievable but has not yet been tested: "A deployable Strategic Defense Initiative appears *practicable* within the next 10 years." *Practical* means known to be useful, effective, sound: "Her analysis of that situation is *practical.*"

precede/proceed/procedure Spelling seems to be a more common problem than usage with these words. Consult a dictionary if you have any doubt. Note the forms of these two:

precede: preceded, preceding.
proceed: proceeded, proceeding, but procedure.

precedence/precedent *Precedence* is simply the act of preceding or coming before. In military communications parlance, the word is used to mean the priority of a message or a telephone call: routine, priority, immediate, or flash precedence. A *precedent* is an established fact or form that serves as a guide thereafter: "The general's use of flash *precedence* on his message set a *precedent* for the traffic that followed."

predominantly/predominately *Predominantly* is preferred.

presently See "at present/currently/presently."

preventative/preventive *Preventive* is preferred.

principal/principle *Principal* is usually an adjective meaning first in authority or importance: "The *principal* architect of the reforms was Mikhail Gorbachev." As a noun it refers either to money ("Spend the interest, not the *principal.*") or to a key person ("Though each team had over 30 members, the *principals* were Dr. Henry Kissinger and Le Duc Tho.") *Principle* is always a noun, never an adjective. It means a standard of conduct, an essential element, or a general truth: "Anwar Sadat was dedicated to the *principle* of peace in the Middle East." "The *principles* of good writing are a *principal* concern at our college."

prioritize Substitute "rank" or another synonym. See also "optimize."

proceed/procedure See "precede/proceed/procedure."

purposefully/purposely *Purposefully* indicates determination to reach a goal: "The United States proceeded *purposefully* with its policy of troop reductions." *Purposely* means intentionally:

"The delegates to the arms control talks *purposely* withheld comment from the press."

qualifiers   Intelligence analysts must often use qualifiers if they are to be objective and accurate. Do not, however, habitually hide judgment behind words such as *apparently, conceivably, evidently, likely, perhaps, possibly, probably, purportedly, reportedly, seemingly, undoubtedly*, and *virtually*. Multiple qualifiers are never justified.

question (as to) whether   When *question* is followed by *whether*, many writers mistakenly insert *as to* between them. Avoid the practice. However, when a noun follows, the phrase "question of" may be used: "The troop movements raised the *question of* the enemy's intentions."

quite   An adverb with shades of meaning for different people. It is usually quite avoidable in intelligence writing.

quota   Means an allotted number, akin to rationing.

quotations   A few tips on quotations: Use them sparingly, but when you use them, use them *correctly* and cite your source appropriately. Be certain to quote material *exactly* when you have it within quotation marks. If your quoted material has an error in it—factual or mechanical—do not correct it; include it as is and put the bracketed expression [*sic*] immediately after it, to tell your reader that it was that way in the original. Use standard double quotation marks (". . .") for short quotations. Use single quotation marks only to show a quotation within a quotation: The Dean said, "The professor told me he is 'the brightest student in the class.' " Notice that periods and commas *always* go inside the final quotation marks, whether or not they are a part of the quoted material. Other punctuation marks go *outside* the quotation marks unless they are a part of the quoted material. Quotations of four typewritten lines or more should be inset and single-spaced. It is not necessary to use quotation marks with an inset quotation; its printed style shows that it is a direct quotation.

range/vary   To *range* is to change or differ within limits: "Elevations *range* between 500 and 1,500 meters above sea level." To *vary* is to change in succession: "Temperatures *vary* from season to season."

recurrence/reoccurrence *Recurrence* has the sense of happening repeatedly or periodically, whereas a *reoccurrence* means a second occurrence. It is redundant to say "another recurrence."

regards to *Regards,* a noun plural, is used to convey good wishes or an expression of affection: "Give my *regards* to the family." *In regards to* is substandard; use *about, on, with regard to,* or *regarding.*

relatively Use only when the intended comparison can be easily grasped: "He has a *relatively* heavy workload." (Relative to what? Last week? His peers?)

represent Means to depict or symbolize, not constitute. Do not write "South African gold *represents* most of the world's output."

reticent Means uncommunicative or reserved; it does not mean reluctant.

sanction As a verb, *sanction* means to authorize, approve, or allow; to ratify or confirm.

saving/savings *Savings* should *not* be used as a singular noun. We may buy a *savings* bond and keep our money in a *savings* bank; but: "The budget reduction would mean an annual *saving* (not savings) of $200,000."

secondly/thirdly Don't "prettify" numbers with the *-ly* suffix. It is unnecessary for the meaning of the sentence.

sector *Sector* is correct in economics or position warfare, but should not be used in political, religious, or sociological contexts. Instead, try *sect, faction, clique, group, side,* or *party.*

sexism See "he or she."

she/her It is no longer preferable to apply these pronouns to countries, although tradition still calls for their use when referring to ships. Use *it* or *its* when referring to a country. "Yugoslavia lost *its* national identity after the Cold War."

ship See "boat/ship."

sic The Latin word *sic* literally means *so* or *thus.* It is handy to use when you are quoting material or citing a source and you find an error or omission in the material you are quoting. To show your reader that your source—and not you—made the error, use a bracketed [*sic*]: One humorist misquoted President

George H. W. Bush's inaugural address by calling for "a thousand pints [*sic*] of light."

sometime/sometimes   *Sometime* is preferred.

south/southern   See "east/eastern." The same principles apply.

Soviet bloc   See "East/Soviet bloc."

stalemate   Chess players will tell you that a stalemate is as final as a checkmate, and cannot be eased, broken, or lifted. If you have in mind an *impasse*, use that word instead.

stanch/staunch   Use *stanch* as a verb meaning to stop the flow of something: "The authorities cannot *stanch* the wave of terrorism in the United States." *Staunch*, an adjective, means loyal, faithful, or strong: "They are *staunch* supporters of more severe penalties for terrorism."

such as   See "like/such as."

tenant/tenet   A *tenant* pays rent; a *tenet* is a principle or guiding thought. "The *Tenants'* Association believed in the *tenet* of service first, rent later."

that/which   *That* is better to introduce a restrictive clause. A restrictive clause narrows the item under consideration from what it would be if the sentence did not contain the clause: "The computer *that* is broken is in the repair shop." Presumably multiple computers are available, and the speaker is focusing on the one that is broken. In contrast, a nonrestrictive clause merely adds information about the set of items under consideration: "The computer, *which* is broken, is in the repair shop." Here the speaker does not narrow the set of items—one computer—but merely provides additional information about it. We also know from that sentence that only one computer is available. Often the "that" in a restrictive clause can be profitably eliminated, making your writing more concise: "The broken computer is in the repair shop."

their/there   *Their* is the plural possessive pronoun, and *there* is usually an adverb but also can be other parts of speech: "*Their* ship is the destroyer in the harbor, over *there*."

there are   Like its singular counterpart *it is*, this phrase usually signals a sentence in need of improvement. (See "it is.")

together with   See "along with."

toward/towards   *Toward* is preferred.

uninterested   See "disinterested."

unique   See "incomparables." If a thing is unique, there is precisely one of it, no more and no less.

unknown   A fact is unknown only if absolutely no one knows about it. Use such terms as *unidentified, undisclosed,* or *undetermined.*

unload   See "offload/unload."

upward/upwards   *Upward* is preferred.

usage/use   Use the shorter form in most instances, except when referring to the way in which language or its elements are used, related, or pronounced.

utilize   Try using the more direct word, *use.*

vary   See "range/vary."

verbal   See "oral/verbal."

very   A *very, very* overworked word. Give it a rest.

viable   *Viable* means workable and likely to survive. It has become a "vogue word" and is commonly used in the sense of workable or achievable. Adjectives such as *durable, lasting, effective,* and *practical* are more appropriate.

vogue words   Vogue words, phrases, or expressions suddenly and inexplicably crop up in speeches of bureaucrats, in comments of columnists, and in broadcasts. These expressions soon become debased by overuse and eventually become obsolete. Even though you may use them regularly in speech, avoid using such phrases as *positive feedback, think outside the box,* and *behind the power curve* in your writing.

waiver/waver   A *waiver* is an intentional relinquishment of some right or interest. To hesitate is to *waver.*

way/ways   *Way* is preferred: "He is a long *way* from home."

weapon/weapons   As an adjective, the singular form is preferable, except in *weapons* carrier, *weapons* selection, *weapons* list, or *weapons* assignment.

west/western   See "east/eastern." The same principles apply.

which   See "that/which."

while   Do not use *while* in the sense of *and,* or *although,* as in: "He spent his youth in Ohio, *while* his father grew up in California." It is not likely that the person in that sentence spent his or her childhood in Ohio *at the same time as* dear old Dad was growing up on the West Coast. *While* refers to time, in the sense of "at the same time as": "I will sauté the onions *while* you marinate the meat."

with Does not have the conjunctive force of *and*. *With* is too often used to attach to a sentence an additional thought that would be better treated as an independent clause preceded by *and* or a semicolon: "English and history are his major subjects, *with* economics as his first elective," should be rewritten: "English and history are his major subjects, *and* economics is his first elective," or "English and history are his major subjects; economics is his first elective."

Note for Chapter 10

1. *The Random House Dictionary of the English Language*, 2d ed., 2000, under the word "hopefully."

Part III

CITATION STYLE AND HANDLING CLASSIFIED MATERIAL

11

Citing Your Sources

Who?

Much of this book has been oriented toward professionals in the intelligence and national security communities. This chapter, however, is intended for a different audience: students—especially those pursuing curricula in intelligence or national security studies. There are occasional references to a thesis for those students whose graduate course of study culminates with the production of that document.

But this material will also be useful for professionals who are pursuing part-time studies or writing articles for refereed journals. The forms and formats prescribed here follow a widely used reference guide and can serve you well in many venues besides academic work.

Why?

Many intelligence analysts are inclined to ask "Why?" when confronted with the dizzying array of forms and formats used to document sources in academic work. After all, they think, we've been writing intelligence reports for years and never had to worry about such things as periods, commas, and hanging indentation. That is true to some extent, but if you really think about it, almost everything you've written has had a prescribed format, some more structured than others. Whether it's a letter to friends or family (snail mail) or an electronic greeting (e-mail), some format is required.

Footnotes (or endnotes) and bibliographies not only show a professor what sources you used in your research but also enable an interested reader to pursue the subject of your paper in future scholarly research. Your professors will specify whether they prefer footnotes or endnotes.

Number footnotes consecutively throughout the paper or the thesis. If you prefer to number the notes by chapter (in a thesis), then use endnotes, and place them at the end of each chapter with the A-level heading "Notes for Chapter *xx*," the "*xx*" being the chapter number. The format, however, is identical for both footnotes and endnotes; only the placement differs. In this book the term "notes" means either footnotes or endnotes.

If you use endnotes for a paper or thesis and include them all at the end of the paper, numbered consecutively throughout, begin them on a separate page after the conclusion of your text. Use the centered, bolded heading "Notes" (not "Endnotes") on the first page of the endnotes. Their placement makes it obvious that they are endnotes.

Many professors—and supervisors—prepare explicit guidelines for what they expect. Read those guidelines carefully before you start work. If, however, you anticipate trying to publish your work, expect some reformatting to accommodate the citation style of your intended publisher.

How?

Academic citation is among the most structured forms you will find, but a few hours spent studying this chapter—especially this first section—will greatly ease your transition into footnotes, endnotes, and bibliographies. Compare similar forms and note how the placement of data is similar: author, title, publication data, and page numbers, for example. As you gather materials for a paper or for your thesis, note the ones you are citing most regularly—probably books, Internet or Intelink sources, journals, magazines, newspapers, and certain types of U.S. Government publications. For those products, set up "template" files by carefully constructing a sample citation for each type of product; then when you have another, simply call up a copy of the template for that form and type over the original data. In an academic year, that will save you many hours of searching this book.

Footnote and bibliographic entries follow a prescribed format. In fact all documentation follows some format. Ours is based on the widely used *Chicago Manual of Style*. Familiarize yourself with that basic format, and then consult this book when you encounter variations. No guide of this size can hope to cover all the variations you will come across. In many cases you will need to extrapolate formats; that is, you might have to find a similar entry and adapt its general guidelines. Adaptations are often a matter of common sense.

General Format

Forms vary widely, depending upon the type of work being cited. Consult the appropriate entry (book, periodical, or U.S. Government publication, for example), and follow its format precisely. Note that commas separate major elements of the note form, whereas periods separate elements of the bibliography. In the bibliography, authors' names are reversed (for alphabetization), but not in the note. If more than one author is listed, reverse only the first-listed author's name in the bibliography. Observe, too, that we italicize the names of major works such as books and periodical titles. All modern printers and word processors support italics; in older publications you might see underlining instead. Underlining and italics are synonymous.

Spacing and Fonts

Space only once after periods. Note forms and bibliographic forms are single-spaced within the entry and double-spaced between entries. Indent notes one tab (approximately one-half inch) on the first line, then leave subsequent lines flush with the left margin. Bibliographic entries are flush with the left margin on the first line, and each subsequent line is "hang-indented" one tab (one-half inch). Some word processors (Microsoft Word, for example) will hang-indent automatically. In the "Format" drop-down menu in Microsoft Word, click "Paragraph," then under the "Indents and Spacing" tab, use the arrow under "Special" to highlight "Hanging." If you have already typed your bibliography without hang-indentation, you can still use that procedure by highlighting the entire bibliography (mouse click-and-drag), then performing the steps above. Just be sure you have used a hard return at the end of each separate bibliography entry but have not included a hard return at the end of the line within an entry.

Throughout this chapter we have formatted our examples using the above guidance. Your footnotes or endnotes should be set in the same font as the rest of your paper, but use a smaller point size for the notes. For example, if you use Times New Roman 11-point (a widely used font), then your notes should be set in Times New Roman 10-point. The bibliography is set in the same size font as the text. In the case of each note form, we have included an example of a secondary (short) citation, representing the way the note would look after the first full citation.

Sample Note and Bibliographic Forms

Microsoft Word is a standard word processor in many organizations and institutions, including within the U.S. Government. "Word" will automatically insert footnotes into your text, but unless you change certain default values, you might have to reformat the notes. With your cursor placed where you want the footnote number to appear, click "Insert" on the menu bar at the top of the page.[1] In the drop-down (cascading) menu, click "Reference," then point to "Footnote." When you click "Footnote," a pop-up box will give you options for placement and numbering. If the default value is what you want (and it probably will be), then click "Insert," and Word will take you to the appropriate setup. It will also insert a superscripted note number in the text where you placed your cursor.

The following is an annotated example of the note and bibliographic forms employed throughout this book. The first entry, "Note Form," shows the way a footnote or endnote for that source would look. The manner of referring to that source again in the same paper is shown next, under "Next Reference to the Same Source." Finally, a sample bibliographic entry for that source is shown.

Note Form

¹Jeffrey Scott Conklin, *Forging an East Asian Foreign Policy* (Lanham, MD: University Press of America, 1995), 22.

The first line of the note is indented, while the second line is flush with the left margin. The note number is superscripted. (If you use endnotes, the numbers will not be superscripted.) The author's name, listed first, is not reversed. The title of the book— a major work—is italicized. Publication data (the place of publication, publisher, and copyright date) are in parentheses, followed by the page number where the information was found. Note that "p." or "pp." abbreviations are not used for page numbers. Commas separate main elements of the note.

Next Reference to the Same Source

²Conklin, 25.

For a subsequent reference to the same source, number the note sequentially. Use only the author's last name and a page number, separated by a comma. If the work you are citing had no author listed, use the title of the work or a short title. See also "Secondary (Short) Citations," later in this section.

Bibliographic Form

> Conklin, Jeffrey Scott. *Forging an East Asian Foreign Policy*. Lanham,
> MD: University Press of America, 1995.

In the bibliography, the font size is the same as the text. The author's name is reversed to facilitate alphabetization, and major elements of the citation are separated by periods. Note that the publication data are not in parentheses for the bibliography, and page numbers are not cited for books. The entry is hang-indented—the second and subsequent lines indented approximately one-half inch.

The remainder of this section applies to note and bibliography forms in general and is intended to answer some of the questions most frequently asked by students. Note that the headings in this section ("Abbreviations," for example) are arranged alphabetically for ease of reference.

Abbreviations

Do not write "p." or "pp." before page numbers in citations, because they are always the last element of a note or bibliographic form. Use "and others" instead of "*et al.*," and use a short citation instead of "*ibid.*" Modern usage is moving away from the Latin abbreviations.

If you are uncertain whether your reader will understand an abbreviation, spell it out the first time you use it. Common abbreviations such as state names, DC (District of Columbia), and GPO (Government Printing Office) may be used without spelling them out first. Note also that our form calls for omission of the periods in these abbreviations, but not in the abbreviation for United States (U.S.).

Use "ed." for editor or edition, "comp." for compiler, and "trans." for translation or translator. Plurals are "eds.," "comps.," and "trans." When no date of publication is given for your source, use "n.d." (no date) in the normal position of the date. When no publication data are provided, use "n.p." (no publisher). You may also omit "Inc.," "Ltd.," or "Co." from publishers' names. See "Publishers" later in this chapter.

Alphabetization

Some ABCs of Alphabetizing

Many word processing programs will alphabetize bibliographies automatically. You must still check these listings, though, because the programs often err. For example, they will alphabetize entries beginning with an article (*a*, *an*, or *the*) under that letter (*a* or *t*) rather than ignoring the article as most style guides—including this one—instruct you to do.

Foreign Names

Many foreign names pose particular problems in alphabetizing. Oriental names, for example, are not reversed in the bibliography. Rather than detail all the rules for each of these name groups, we invite you to consult *The Chicago Manual of Style* (15th edition) or the 7th edition of Kate Turabian's *A Manual for Writers*, both of which are available in most libraries.

Alphabetizing Numbers

Alphabetize numbers in the bibliography *before* the alphabetical listing. For example, if you used sources from the 1st Cavalry Division, 3d Marine Expeditionary Force, 7th Fleet, and 17th Air Force, those entries would be placed at the start of your bibliography, in the same ascending order as shown in this sentence. For purposes of sequencing, treat Roman numerals as Arabic numbers: V U.S. Corps, for example, would be listed as 5th (V) U.S. Corps.

Anonymous Authors or Unattributed Work

It is not unusual to find articles and editorials that do not identify the author. In such cases, do not use the words "anonymous," "author unknown," or "unattributed." Such works are alphabetized by the first word of the title or, if the first word is an article (*a*, *an*, or *the*), alphabetical placement is determined by the first word following it. Do note, though, that this rule pertains to titles in English only. Foreign titles are alphabetized by the first word of the title, even if it is an article, preposition, or conjunction: An article entitled "The Washington Beltway Syndrome," with no listed author, is alphabetized under *W*, but the German magazine title *Der Spiegel* (translated as "the mirror"), if it is the first element of your citation, is alphabetized under *D*. (See "Foreign Publications.")

Capitalization and Punctuation in Titles

Often the titles of books, magazine articles, or newspaper articles will use nonstandard capitalization or will have no punctuation between the title and the subtitle. In those cases, standardize the capitalization and punctuation, following the examples.

> Book Title on Cover: *INDONESIA a country study*
>   Standardized for Note or Bibliography: *Indonesia: A Country Study*
> Newspaper Article—Headline Followed by Subhead:
>   "Iraq dominates bar conversation
>   Customers back Bush, GIs in war"
> Standardized for Note or Bibliography:
>   "Iraq Dominates Bar Conversation: Customers Back Bush, GIs in War"

Cited Hereafter as . . .

Remember to avoid Latin abbreviations such as *ibid.* and *op. cit.* Instead, in the note form, use the last name of the author, agency, or organization, followed by a page number. See also "Secondary (Short) Citations." In some cases, especially long or complex entries, you might want to abbreviate organizations or other elements of the note for a secondary citation. To be sure that your reader understands what you are doing, add the words "Cited hereafter as . . ." to the end of the first citation of the source, as in the example that follows. For simple citations that are not likely to cause confusion—authored books or articles, for example—you don't need to use this tag.

[1]Stanford Central American Action Network (SCAAN), *Revolution in Central America* (Boulder, CO: Westview Press, 1983), 468. Cited hereafter as SCAAN.

Dates of Publication

General

The date to be used in citing a source is usually the copyright date. It is found either on the cover, on the title page, on the back of the title page, or a combination of those three places. Look for the date following the copyright symbol: © 2009. If more than one copyright date is listed, use the most recent. Ignore "printing" dates—use copyright date. Dates of periodicals are usually on the cover or first page. If the date is shown, for example, as March 21, 2003, then standardize it for your citation as 21 March 2003. Always spell out the month in both note and bibliographic forms.

No Date Listed ("n.d.")

Some products—especially electronic sources and unpublished works—have no discernible publication date. In that case, use "n.d." (no date) in the normal position of the date. Since it follows a comma, both letters are lowercase.

Epigraphs

Many writers like to begin papers or chapters with a relevant quotation, called an "epigraph," also called—with tongue in cheek—"dead man quotes." Epigraphs are neither indented nor enclosed in quotation marks. The author of the quotation and the source are given below the epigraph, flush right. No other documentation is needed. The epigraph itself is single-spaced. Finally, the epigraph that heads a whole paper and occupies a page by itself should not be included in the table of contents, and the page should not be numbered.

An example of an epigraph from the master's thesis of Captain Steve Magnan, USAF, is shown. Captain Magnan was a student in the 1998 Postgraduate Intelligence Program at the Joint Military Intelligence College (now the National Defense Intelligence College) in Washington, DC. Note its spacing: The epigraph begins one double space beneath the chapter title and is itself single-spaced. Text of the paper (or the first A-level heading) would appear one double space beneath the last line of the epigraph—in this case, the source of the quotation.

Chapter 2

Information Technology Impact

Unless soldiers and statesmen, diplomats and arms control negotiators, peace activists and politicians understand what lies ahead, we may find ourselves fighting—or preventing—the wars of the past, rather than those of tomorrow.
—Alvin and Heidi Toffler, *War and Anti-War*

Explanatory Notes

You might want to include information that seems important for your reader to know but does not seem to fit or seem important enough to be in the text of your paper or thesis. A good way to handle this sort of information is to write an explanatory note, also called a substantive or content note.

Explanatory notes also may be used to define terms or to provide additional commentary that does not fit into the text of your paper. If you find an explanatory note growing to the size of a hefty paragraph, chances are you have developed a main point that may deserve its own place in the text of your paper. Use explanatory notes sparingly, and do not yield to the temptation to include really useless information that you have come across. This may seem obvious, but there is a scholarly compulsion to want to include as much as possible of what one has dug up in the research process. Successful writing draws some of its strength from selectivity, so be selective in writing the text of your paper and in your use of explanatory notes. See also "Multiple Sources in One Note."

Observe how Captain Magnan uses this form in his thesis, *Information Operations: Are We Our Own Worst Enemy?* when he discusses poor security practices:

> Even more simplistic, yet not vigilantly followed, are protective measures surrounding DoD recycling programs and trash. Even with the advent of computer technology, vast amounts of information can still be gathered by the age-old art of "dumpster-diving."[37]

Magnan then uses an explanatory note to define the term he has used and to provide additional clarification that might be awkward in the text:

> [37]"Dumpster-diving" is a term used to describe information and data gathered from literally sorting through another organization's trash. Hackers still use this technique to gather passwords, modem phone numbers, and other such necessary items they need to successfully "break in." However, many others sort through trash and find even more sensitive information as cited in [the earlier] example.

Although this additional information may not be significant enough to include in the text, it provides a point of interest and shows that Magnan has researched many different elements of his topic.

Other Relevant Sources

You might want to use an explanatory note to refer your reader to other relevant sources. (See also the paragraph later in this chapter entitled "Multiple Sources in One Note.") Samuel P. Huntington, in his article "Coping with the Lippman Gap," refers readers in this note[2] to other writers who have discussed Lippman's view of foreign policy balance (note Huntington's use of semicolons between sources):

[2]For other discussions of the Lippman Gap problem see Joseph S. Nye Jr., "U.S. Power and Reagan Policy," *Orbis* (Summer 1982): 391–411; Jeffrey Record, *Revising U.S. Military Strategy: Tailoring Means to Ends* (Washington, DC: Pergamon-Brassey, 1984); Eliot A. Cohen, "When Policy Outstrips Power," *Public Interest* (Spring 1984): 3–19; and David C. Hendrickson, *The Future of American Strategy* (New York: Holmes and Meier, 1987).

Personal Experience

Finally, an explanatory note is a good device to use when you want to cite yourself—that is, when you want to refer to your own experience with the subject you are discussing, perhaps to add credibility to your argument. That type of note might take the form shown:

[1]Unless otherwise noted, material in this section is based on the author's personal experience as Commander of the 109th Reconnaissance Company during Operation IRAQI FREEDOM from March through July 2003.

Foreign-Language Publications

If you read a foreign language, you might have occasion to use publications printed in that language. Similar documentation requirements apply, but you must make it clear when you translate material that any such translation is clearly noted as yours. In the following example, an article from the German-language magazine *Der Spiegel*, you translated the title of the article. Some style manuals use something like "Translation by the author"; but when you cite an authored article like the example, the reader might mistakenly conclude that the author of the article did the translation. Accordingly, this is one of those rare instances where you may use the first person: "Translation is mine." If, however, you make extensive use of foreign-language materials—in a thesis or final course paper, for example—you might wish to place a preface early in your work, explaining that unless otherwise noted, translations are yours. Show the translated words in parentheses.

¹Romain Leick, "Langer Marsch" ("Long March"), *Der Spiegel*, 10 March 2003, 154. Translation is mine.

Indirect (Secondary) References

General

It is always a good idea to go directly to a source rather than to quote that source from someone else's work. Occasionally, however, you might need to quote or cite one author as found in another author's work; for example, the work cited by an author might be out of print. Provide information on both the original and your own source in the note form. The bibliographic entry will be for your source only. If at all possible, though, the thorough researcher will secure the original.

Book (or Report) Cited in a Book

In the first example, the student is citing a source that she found on page 116 of Summers' book. The original source, Admiral Sharp's report, had the information on page 6. Here the student used more than one source by Harry Summers, so she used a short title for Summers' book in the secondary citation. To emphasize Sharp's report rather than Summers' book, see the next entry.

Note Form

¹Admiral U.S.G. Sharp, USN, "Report on Air and Naval Campaigns Against North Vietnam and Pacific Command-wide Support of the War, June 1964–July 1968," Report on the War in Vietnam (Washington, DC: GPO, 1968), 6, quoted in Harry G.

Summers Jr., *On Strategy: A Critical Analysis of the Vietnam War* (Novato, CA: Presidio Press, 1982), 116.

Next Reference to the Same Source

²Sharp, quoted in Summers, *On Strategy*, 117.

Bibliographic Form

Summers, Harry G. Jr. *On Strategy: A Critical Analysis of the Vietnam War*. Novato, CA: Presidio Press, 1982.

Lecture, Cited in a Book

Note that these forms emphasize Kennan's lecture, and not Gaddis's book, in which the lecture was cited. In the bibliographic entry, cite the inclusive pages where the lecture is quoted.

Note Form

³George Kennan, lecture presented at the National War College, 18 December 1947, quoted in John Louis Gaddis, *Strategies of Containment: A Critical Appraisal of Postwar National Security Policy* (Oxford: Oxford University Press, 1982), 42.

Next Reference to the Same Source

⁴Kennan lecture, quoted in Gaddis, 43.

Bibliographic Form

Kennan, George. Lecture presented at the National War College, 18 December 1947. Quoted in John Louis Gaddis, *Strategies of Containment: A Critical Appraisal of Postwar National Security Policy*. Oxford: Oxford University Press, 1982, 42–43.

Members of Congress

To cite a member of Congress as a source, include his or her party affiliation and home state, using standard abbreviations for both, as shown in the example. If your document does not show that information, look it up in a reference book such as *United States Government Organization Manual*, *Official Congressional Directory*, or a current annual publication such as *The World Almanac*. In the example, Congressman (Rep.) Lee H. Hamilton is a Democrat (D) from Indiana (IN). Use the letter "R" for Republicans, and standard two-letter postal state abbreviations, which are listed in chapter 8, "Abbreviations."

Note Form

[1]Rep. Lee H. Hamilton (D-IN), "F-15 Enhancement Package for Saudi Arabia," *Congressional Record* (6 May 1981), vol. 127, pt. 3, 8739–8741.

Bibliographic Form

Hamilton, Lee H., Rep. (D-IN). "F-15 Enhancement Package for Saudi Arabia." *Congressional Record* (6 May 1981), vol. 127, pt. 3.

Military Rank

Documenting Sources

Include military rank when it is part of your source documentation. Use the forms shown. It is also helpful (but not required) to add the individual's title. Note that the second examples for the note and bibliographic forms that follow are for a foreign military officer. Note also that there is no comma before "II" in the first source or "Jr." in the second entry. (See "Titles," later in this chapter.)

Note Form

    ¹General John R. Smith II, USA (Ret.), CINCUSEUCOM from 1998–2000, interview by the author, 27 February 2003.

Bibliographic Form

    Smith, John R. II, General, USA (Ret.). CINCUSEUCOM from 1998–2000. Interview by the author, 27 February 2003.

Note Form (Second Example)

    ²Air Marshal Jonathan Witherspoon-Smythe Jr., British Army, Commander IFOR Panaragua, 1997, interview by the author, 11 March 2009.

Bibliographic Form (Second Example)

    Witherspoon-Smythe, Jonathan Jr., Air Marshal, British Army. Commander IFOR Panaragua, 1997. Interview by the author, 11 March 2009.

Military Ranks with Abbreviations

Follow appropriate style for abbreviating military ranks, as listed in chapter 8.

Military Titles: References in the Text

At times you will refer to a military title (rank or grade) in the text of your paper. If you use the individual's full name, then abbreviate the title: "LTG John J. Ranger, USA, took command in April." If you use the surname alone, then spell out the title: "In a recent interview, Lieutenant General Ranger cited the contributions made by his intelligence staff."

Missing Data

Many students have come to me over the years with citation questions. Occasionally a student will bring in a piece of paper or even a stack of papers and ask: "How do I cite this?" "This" turns out to be a download from the Internet. It has no title, no author, and no publisher listed. My initial reaction is usually not *how* to cite that source but rather "*Why* cite it?" In an academic paper, you and your reader need some assurance of the validity of your information and the reliability of your source. Except for a Uniform Resource Locator (URL) or a homepage, many World Wide Web sources fail that simple test.

There are, however, many occasions when you will find elements of the source data missing. Newspaper editorials, for example, usually list no authors; neither do some magazine articles. Government publications often do not clearly show a publisher, place of publication, or even a date. How to handle those legitimate cases is shown elsewhere in these pages. (See, for example, "Publishers.") However, when you can, try to find out as much as possible about your sources. That is a goal for students and intelligence professionals alike.

Multiple Sources in One Note

General

On occasion you might find it necessary to cite two or more sources in the same note. In addition, you may wish to add some explanation to a note. Either of those cases may be handled as shown.[3] Note the semicolons between major entries in the first example. Note in the second example how Captain Ford uses a short citation for Wirtz's book, which he had cited fully in an earlier footnote.

The entry shown as "Next Reference to the Same Source"— the secondary citation—assumes that you cited all of the same sources, including the same page numbers, in a previous note.

The second such entry assumes that you used different page numbers in two of the four works cited. A secondary citation is not shown for the second example because you do not need a secondary reference for that note. In addition, a bibliographic entry is not shown for either example, because you must cite each item separately in the bibliography, using standard citation format. See also the information under "Explanatory Notes" earlier in this chapter.

Note Form

[1]Stanley Karnow, *Vietnam: A History* (New York: Penguin Books, 1991), 528–81; George C. Herring, *America's Longest War: The United States in Vietnam, 1950–1975* (New York: Knopf Publishers, 1986), 186–220; William S. Turley, *The Second Indochina War: A Short Political and Military History, 1954–1975* (New York: Westview Press, 1986), 99–119; and James J. Wirtz, *The Tet Offensive: Intelligence Failure in War* (Ithaca, NY: Cornell University Press, 1991).

Next Reference to the Same Source

This example shows a secondary citation for the above note when all information in the note remains exactly the same.

[2]Karnow and others.

Next Reference

This shows a secondary citation for the above note when some of the information changes—in this case, the page numbers.

[3]Karnow, 573; Herring, 186–220; Turley, 99–119; Wirtz, 35.

Note Form

This example is a combination of an explanatory note and additional source material relevant to the information being cited.

[4]For thoroughly researched and documented evidence that indicators of an impending communist attack were in the hands of allied intelligence prior to the Tet Offensive, see Wirtz, *The Tet Offensive*; Glen Helm, *The Tet 1968 Offensive: A Failure of Allied Intelligence*, MMAS Thesis (Tempe, AZ: Arizona State University, 1989); and Hoang Ngoc Lung, *The General Offensives of 1968–69* (Washington, DC: U.S. Army Center for Military History, 1981).

Names, Referenced in the Text

When you refer to someone repeatedly in the text of your paper, it helps readability if you vary the reference periodically. For example, if you are reviewing the published works of Dr. Richard D. Lionhearted and you mention him four times in succession, your paragraph might look something like this (the italicized feature simply points out the references and should not be used in your paper):

> Among noted scholars who have written on Kenya, *Dr. Richard D. Lionhearted* stands out. *His* works have appeared in many publications, including encyclopedias and scholarly journals. *Lionhearted*, fluent in Swahili, has translated African literature for English-speaking audiences. This thesis will make extensive use of *Dr. Lionhearted's* materials in the thesis chapter dealing with ethnic rivalries in central Kenya.

Periodicals

General

As their name suggests, periodicals are products that are published periodically—usually daily, weekly, biweekly, or monthly. The most frequently encountered periodicals include digests, journals, magazines, and newspapers.

Titles of Periodicals

Periodical titles are italicized, and titles of articles or segments within them are enclosed in quotation marks. A standard convention in notes and bibliographies is to omit an initial article in a periodical title; for example, *The Washington Post* and *The Washington Times* are cited simply as *Washington Post* and *Washington Times* in a footnote or bibliography. In the text, however, you might use that initial "The," depending upon context. The ear is often a good judge:

> *The Washington Post* criticized efforts being made. . . .
> *Washington Times* reporter Bill Gertz wrote. . . .

Article Titles and Subtitles

Many articles in periodicals have not only a title (often called a headline) but also a subtitle (also known as a subhead or subheading). For example, an 11 April 2008 *Washington Times* article by Audrey Hudson on page A1 has this headline: "Airport Watch List Now Reviewed Often." The subhead beneath that headline reads: "Thousands Not Terror Suspects." You are not required to include subheads of periodical articles in your citation, but if you do, separate the title from the subtitle with a colon, as follows: "Airport Watch List Now Reviewed Often: Thousands Not Terror Suspects." As you see, that can make for some long citations. But if you do it for one, do it for all. See also "Capitalization and Punctuation in Titles" earlier in this chapter.

Publishers

No Publisher Listed ("n.p.")

If no publication data are given on the cover, title page, or elsewhere in your source, use "n.p." (no publisher) in its place. The first letter of the abbreviation ("n.") is lowercase in the note form, because it follows a comma. In bibliographic forms, however, where it follows a period or a colon, the letter "N" is capitalized— but not the letter "p."

Publishers' Names

Always cite the name of the publisher exactly as it appears on the title page. In the publisher's name, you may omit words such as Company (Co.), Incorporated (Inc.), and Limited (Ltd.) from the citation. If more than one city is named for the publisher, use only the first one listed. Carefully note any unusual spelling or capitalization, and retain it exactly; for example: *Encyclopaedia Britannica* and *Jane's Defence Weekly* (British spellings); and Macmillan Publishing (the second *m* is lower case).

State, Province, Territory, and District Names

For place of publication in your note and bibliography entries, use the U.S. Postal Service two-letter abbreviations, which are listed in chapter 8, "Abbreviations." Do not abbreviate the names, however, in the text of your papers.

U.S. Government Documents

U.S. Government documents are usually published by the command, agency, or organization listed on the front cover or title page. For example, Defense Intelligence Agency (DIA) products carry a Publication Control Number (PCN) on the back cover, showing that DIA published that document. (The second edition of the book *Clift Notes*, for example, has PCN 43713 on the back cover.) If that distinction is unclear, look in the margins of the last few pages of the product. You will often find a "U.S. Government Printing Office" control number there. In that case, list GPO as the publisher.

Punctuation

General

Separate major elements of note forms (footnotes and end-notes) by commas:

[1]Author, *Title of Major Work Italicized* (Place of Publication: Publisher, date), page number.

Note that no punctuation precedes the parentheses in any note form, and that the place of publication is separated from the publisher by a colon. In the bibliography, major elements are separated by periods:

Author with name reversed. *Title of Major Work Italicized.* Place of publication: Publisher, date.

This section deals with punctuation problems you might face in citing your sources. For more detail on punctuation marks in general, see chapter 6, "Punctuation."

Punctuation within Punctuation

You will occasionally have a citation where you must use punctuation within punctuation—most often, quotation marks or italics.

Quotation Marks within Quotation Marks

Remember that the only time you will use single quotation marks is within double quotation marks. This might happen when the source you are citing already uses quotation marks. For example, in the headline of the newspaper article that follows, the words "Not Reasonable" were in quotation marks. In the citation, therefore, those words are in single quotation marks, because the title of the article is enclosed in double quotation marks:

Bibliographic Form

> Lynch, Colum. "Ending Inspections 'Not Reasonable,' Blix Says." *Washington Post*, 19 March 2003, A17.

Italics within Italics

If a word or words in the title of a major work are italicized or underlined, simply remove the italics or underlining from the word or words in your citation. For example, in the bibliographic citation that follows, the name of the newspaper (*Times*, *New York Times*) is italicized twice on the title page of the book:

Bibliographic Form

> Diamond, Edwin. *Behind the* Times: *Inside the* New York Times. Chicago: University of Chicago Press, 1995.

"Stacked" Punctuation

If the title of a source you are citing ends with a punctuation mark (for example, a question mark or exclamation point), then do not "stack" punctuation by following the title with a comma (in the note form) or a period (in the bibliography), as you would normally do. For example, in the following bibliographic entry, the book's title would typically be followed by a period. Since the title ends with an exclamation point, however, the period is omitted.

Bibliographic Form

> Shaw, Harry. *Punctuate It Right!* New York: Harper & Row, Publishers, 1963.

Punctuation in Quoted Material

Any material that you quote verbatim in your paper must be cited properly, including its punctuation and its style. For proper use of quotation marks, see the discussion of that topic in chapter 6,

"Punctuation." The most common marks of punctuation you will use within quoted material are brackets and ellipses. Each is discussed in chapter 6.

Block Quotations

Use a block quotation when the material you are quoting is four lines or more of typescript. The block quotation is indented one tab from the left margin and runs flush with the right margin. Do not indent on both sides. If the block quotation begins with a paragraph in the original, indent the first line an additional tab.

Do not place quotation marks around the material; your reader knows you are quoting because of the indentation and single-spacing. If, however, you have an interior quotation (as in the example "Extract from a Thesis"), mark it with double quotation marks, not single.[4] Note that the text of the example is double-spaced, and the block quotation is single-spaced. The font size is the same as the text.

A colon or other punctuation may be used to introduce the quoted material, unless it is a "run-on" quotation like the example. A run-on quotation continues the flow of the sentence with no noticeable pause. Note also that we have omitted a portion of Captain Don's quotation—shown by the ellipsis—and have changed the case of the word "our" from lowercase to uppercase, using brackets.

Because block quotations are long, use them sparingly. They should, like the following example, contain striking words or phrases that would be difficult or not worthwhile to paraphrase.

Extract from a Thesis, Showing a Block Quotation

In reference to current and future threats, General Peter J. Schoomaker, Commander in Chief, United States Special Operations Command (USSOCOM), explains that

> we face threats of a new dimension, different from and more complex than the threat posed by the old Soviet Union. . . . [O]ur most likely adversaries will be rapidly evolving nonstate aggressors such as terrorist organiza-

tions, crime syndicates, drug cartels, and extremist groups who operate "in the seam" between war and crime.[5]

Integrating Quoted Material Smoothly

Whether you insert verbatim or summarize the idea of another person, introduce material smoothly into the text of your paper. Prepare your reader with either a conversational tag or a lead-in sentence. When you employ these devices, avoid the temptation to use verbs of emotion to characterize the quotation; that is, don't say, "The President *felt* that Putin needed to investigate the matter," or "Mr. Fleischer *sensed* that something was wrong." Of course, if you interview the President and he says that he "felt" that way, and Mr. Fleischer tells you he "sensed" it, then you may use those terms. Note the conversational tag and the lead-in sentence in the examples shown, both using, again, the previously quoted material. As with any quoted material, you would of course footnote the quotation.

Conversational Tag

As White House spokesman Ari Fleischer noted, "We are very concerned that there are reports of ongoing cooperation and support to Iraqi military forces being provided by a Russian company that produces GPS-jamming equipment."

Lead-in Sentence

White House spokesman Ari Fleischer noted the President's concern about "ongoing cooperation and support to Iraqi military forces being provided by a Russian company that produces GPS-jamming equipment."

Secondary (Short) Citations

After your first reference to a work in a footnote or endnote, use a secondary citation (also called a short citation or short form) with only the author's last name and a page number. If you use more than one work by the same author, agency, or organization, use a short title in each subsequent reference. Avoid Latin abbreviations such as *ibid.* and *op. cit.* See the examples that follow.

The first example assumes you used only one work by Douglass.

First Reference

> [1]Joseph D. Douglass Jr., *Soviet Military Strategy in Europe* (New York: Pergamon Press, 1980), 198–99.

Next Reference

> [2]Douglass Jr., 202.

The next example assumes you used more than one work by the Central Intelligence Agency. Use enough data in the secondary citation to identify the work clearly for your reader. Notice that by employing the "Cited hereafter as . . ." tag, you make it easier for the reader.

First Reference

> [1]Central Intelligence Agency, "Contemporary Soviet Propaganda and Disinformation: A Conference Report," Airlie, VA, 25–27 June 1985 (Washington, DC: GPO, 1987), 312. Cited hereafter as CIA, "Conference Report."

Next Reference

> [2]CIA, "Conference Report," 313.

First Reference

This next example is one with no author listed. It is a hypothetical newspaper article drawn from wire service reports and carried on several nonsequential pages in the paper. The example assumes that you used no other material with the same title; otherwise, you would have to provide enough data to clarify which entry you are citing.

[1]"New Council Eases Concerns in Baghdad," *Washington Post*, 13 June 2003, final edition, A16+.

Next Reference

[2]"New Council," A24.

Subsequent Works by the Same Author, Agency, or Organization

If you list two or more works in your bibliography by the same author, agency, or organization, give the full name in the first entry only. Thereafter use an eight-space line (the underline key struck eight times) followed by a period. Note that this instruction applies only to bibliographies, not to note forms. Alphabetize these bibliographic entries by title, without regard to initial articles (*a, an, the*). For example:

> Sayigh, Yusif A. *The Determinants of Arab Economic Development.* London: Croom Helm, 1978.
> ———. *Economies of the Arab World: Development Since 1945.* London: Croom Helm, 1978.

Titles of Individuals

Sources are often identified by a title such as Mr., Mrs., Ms., Dr., Jr., Sr. II, III, and the like. Citing these sources in a note or bibliography, you may omit "Mr.," "Mrs.," or "Ms." Treat the title "Dr." as you would a military rank (see that subject earlier in this chapter), substituting "Ph.D." or other title as appropriate ("Ed.D." or "D.B.A.," for example). When the source is a "Junior" (Jr.), "the Second" (II), "the Third" (III), or the like, note the punctuation in the example that follows. Never spell out "Junior," "Second," or "Third." See also "Names, Referenced in the Text," earlier in this chapter.

Note Form

[1]John R. Smith II, Ph.D., interview by the author, 27 February 2003.

Bibliographic Form

Smith, John R. II, Ph.D. Interview by the author, 27 February 2003.

Note Form

[2]Air Marshal Jonathan Witherspoon-Smythe Jr., British Army, Commander IFOR Panaragua, 1997, interview by the author, 11 March 2003.

Bibliographic Form

Witherspoon-Smythe, Jonathan Jr., Air Marshal, British Army. Commander IFOR Panaragua, 1997. Interview by the author, 11 March 2003.

Translation from a Foreign Language

If you translate works you read, then you must note that the translation is yours. A parenthetic notation in the text can do that: "General Nasution's most ambitious work was the two-volume set *Tentara Nasional Indonesia* (*Indonesian National Army*; translation is mine), published in 1968." You may do the same thing in a footnote. See also "Foreign-Language Publications," earlier in this chapter.

Volume Numbers in Notes and Bibliography

Many publications (especially periodicals) give the volume number in Roman numerals: *Parameters* XXXII, no. 2 (Summer 2002). Use Arabic numerals instead of Roman numerals for volume numbers, even if the volume number of your source is given as a Roman numeral: *Parameters* 32, no. 2 (Summer 2002). Do not use the word "volume" or the abbreviation "vol." in periodical references.

Bits and Bytes

Examples shown in this chapter all refer to sources in print or to people you have interviewed. But far more common these days are the overwhelming numbers of sources available from electronic media, especially the Internet. Increasingly, periodicals and even books are published in electronic formats. Some have both a print version and an online version. So how does one go about considering and citing electronic sources? That is the subject of our next chapter.

Notes for Chapter 11

1. These instructions are for the 2003 version of Microsoft Word used by the author at the time of this writing. Earlier or later versions might differ slightly.

2. Samuel P. Huntington, "Coping with the Lippman Gap," *Foreign Affairs* 66, no. 3 (1988): 454.

3. Both examples are taken from Ronnie E. Ford, *Tet 1968: Understanding the Surprise*, Master's Thesis (Washington, DC: Joint Military Intelligence College, 1993).

4. This example is taken from Captain Peter J. Don, USA, *The Awakening: Developing Military Intelligence Professionals to Support United States Army Special Forces*, Master's Thesis (Washington, DC: Joint Military Intelligence College, 1998), 2.

5. General Peter J. Schoomaker, USA, "Special Operations," *Army* (April 1998): 19.

12

Electronic Citations

General

The ubiquitous home computer is leading to a proliferation of services that offer retrievable data online to home subscribers. Academic institutions worldwide are struggling with proper citation formats for electronic material from the Internet and, in the case of the Intelligence Community, from Intelink. We offer here some citation formats, but expect adaptations concurrent with the exponential growth of electronically accessible information.

In the electronic world and in printed material about electronic media, you will encounter many variations in capitalization, hyphenation, compounding, and even spelling. For standardization in our lexicon, we offer the following usages:

Use ...	Not ...
database	data base or data-base
e-mail	email
homepage	home page or home-page
Intelink	INTELINK or Intellink
Internet	internet
online	on-line or on line
website	web site or Website
World Wide Web	Worldwide Web

When you retrieve information electronically, it is important to note the electronic medium (Internet address, for example) and the date you accessed it. Because electronic information tends to be perishable, print out any material you cite in a paper or thesis—at least a page or two for posterity. If you cannot find a citation format to cover your item, extrapolate from one you find here or consult the *Chicago Manual of Style* or Kate Turabian's *Manual for Writers*.

Note also that anyone with a home computer and a modem can place material on the Internet—it is an "information dumpster." So it behooves the careful researcher always to cross-check or verify information from an online source. Your best bet, whenever possible, is to obtain a hard copy (printed version) of anything you cite from the Internet. That applies especially to periodicals, whose online editions often rush to distribute a story—only to retract or change it later.

Electronic Sources

Generally, sources fall into two categories—items published in standard (paper) format and then made available electronically, and items that exist only electronically. In both cases, citations should indicate the electronic address where you accessed the document and the date on which you accessed it, because electronically stored and retrieved items are liable to change. If applicable, include the link in quotation marks or the homepage in italics. An important consideration for dealing with electronic information is to consider what it is that you are citing. Are you using a book? An online edition of a newspaper, magazine, or journal? An e-mail interview? By first determining the nature of your source, you can then cite it just as you would a paper copy of that source, followed by the electronic address of the material and the date you accessed it.

Uniform Resource Locators (URLs)

Note that URLs, the unique electronic "address" of a website, are to be enclosed in angle brackets like the example that follows:

URL: <http://www.dia.mil/jmic/writing_center>. Some word processing programs will automatically convert material contained within angle brackets to a hyperlink, making the URL impossible to edit—in addition to changing the font color and underlining the entry. The underlining makes it difficult to read some elements of a URL, especially if it contains an underscore, such as the URL above.

Look at that same URL, underlined, and note how difficult it is to read the underscore, possibly leading to confusion in trying to access that website: <http://www.dia.mil/jmic/ writing_center>. Note also that the "j" in "jmic" is more difficult to read. Therefore, that feature should be turned off, using the backspace key or the "Undo Typing" arrow on the standard toolbar immediately after the final angle bracket, or by going into the "Format" menu and unchecking it for the whole document.

You will find it necessary to edit URLs, especially in footnotes and bibliographic entries, where the word processor treats the entire URL as one word and "wraps" it to the next line, leaving a wide open white space in your citation. Note the following footnote, with the URL unedited and the ugly white space resulting:

> [16]General Ronald R. Fogelman, Chief of Staff USAF, "Information Operations: The Fifth Dimension of Warfare," transcription of remarks delivered to the Armed Forces Communications-Electronics Association, Washington, DC, 25 April 1995, printed in *Defense Issues* 10, no. 47 (Washington, DC: DoD, 1995), URL: <http://www.dtic.dla.mil/defenselink/pubs/di95/di1047.html>, accessed 31 October 2007.

Now look at the same footnote, where the student disabled the hyperlink, which removed the underline and shaded font, enabling him to edit the URL by breaking it after a punctuation mark:

> [16]General Ronald R. Fogelman, Chief of Staff USAF, "Information Operations: The Fifth Dimension of Warfare," transcription of remarks delivered to the Armed Forces Communications-Electronics Association, Washington, DC, 25 April 1995, printed in *Defense*

Issues 10, no. 47 (Washington, DC: DoD, 1995), URL:<http://www
.dtic.dla.mil/defenselink/pubs/di95/di1047.html>, accessed 31
October 1999.

It might require a couple of "trial-and-error" edits before you
find the right place to break the URL; but generally you can
"eyeball" how much of the text will fit into the blank space. Then
simply place your cursor after a punctuation mark (slash or period, for example) and tap the space bar. If the text does not
"wrap" to fill the white space, then backspace once to remove
the space you just inserted, and move left to the next punctuation mark.

One recognized advantage of retaining the hyperlink, of
course, is that it makes your original source immediately accessible from an electronic copy of your paper. If you wish to have
that option, then you might save a separate electronic copy of
your work.

The Mysterious Disappearing Website

You have probably had occasion to seek access to a website referenced in a book, article, thesis, or other source. Armed with its URL,
you diligently enter all the characters: <http:// www.gpoaccess
.gov/nara/v39no15.cgi-bin/getdoc.cgi?dbname=2003_presden
tial_ documents&docid=pd14ap03_txt-6>. You press "Go" or the
"Enter" key, and after a nanosecond or two you see an all-too-
familiar screen: "The page cannot be displayed."

Inability to access a website derives from two major causes:
(1) You might have made an error in one or more keystrokes. If
you type "presidential_document" instead of "presidential_doc-
uments" in the address above, or if you use a hyphen instead of
an underscore, your browser will not recognize the URL. (2) The
address no longer exists. Some websites remain accessible for
only a set period—days, weeks, or months; many are then
archived and are still retrievable; still others disappear forever
into the Internet ether.

So what can you do to search for your desired document, or at least one like it? One technique is to go to the basic Internet address of the site. For example, in the query above, you would enter: <http://www.gpoaccess.gov/nara>. That address takes you to the homepage of the National Archives and Records Administration and the Federal Register. From that screen you can link to many related documents, including the one you were seeking above, the *Weekly Compilation of Presidential Documents.*

There is actually a real advantage to using the basic address instead of trying to replicate a long, complex alphanumeric string in a directory path. That "homepage" usually offers links to many related documents and other websites. Your research might benefit a great deal by pursuing that broader perspective.

Page Numbers in Electronic Citations

Most electronically-derived items have no page numbers, or pagination differs depending upon the print medium. Your goal is to make the item accessible, so use a section subheading or other identifying data in the page number position. Failing that, leave the page number position blank. Your supervisors and professors understand that electronic material is usually without page numbers. See the exception immediately below.

PDFs, PROQUEST®, TIFFs, and Such

There are exceptions to the "no page number" situation with electronically-derived materials. The most well known include Portable Document Format (PDF), the ProQuest information retrieval system, and Tag(ged) Image File Format (TIFF). When you access information on files of this nature, you are looking at a digitized image of the product. Page numbers, along with all other elements needed for a proper citation, are there. So treat these sources as invisible. Cite the product as though you were looking at it. In essence, you are.

Links, Homepages, and Service Providers

In working with material derived electronically, provide sufficient information for your reader to locate the material later. Keep one guiding principle in mind: If your reader can't potentially retrieve your source, then you can't use it. In some cases, rather than a complex URL that risks failure if one character or punctuation mark is incorrect, it is acceptable—even preferable—to cite only a "link" or a "homepage." For our purposes, a homepage is an opening screen of a work. Picture the homepage as the filing cabinet where the material is stored. A link is a "button" (a hyperlink) that enables you to move directly to another site. Picture it as a drawer within the filing cabinet.

The place to use this technique would be when you cite a major Internet Service Provider such as America Online. An example of such a footnote is shown, where America Online (shown in italics) is the service provider (Version 8.0) and "Research & Learn" is the link, enclosed in quotation marks. Readers who access the "Research & Learn" link would then look for the link to "Encyclopedia." A similar technique is used for dictionaries retrieved from Intelink.

[1]*World Book Encyclopedia*, online edition, under "El Salvador," *America Online* 8.0, "Research & Learn—Encyclopedia" link, accessed 7 February 2008.

Generic Citation Format

Sample generic formats for two of the most common types of electronic citations are shown. A secondary citation format ("Next Reference to the Same Source") is not shown because they vary so widely.

Authored Work Online

Note Form

> [1]Author, "Minor Work Title in Quotation Marks," *Major Work Italicized*, date of item if provided, URL: <in angle brackets>, date you accessed it.

Bibliographic Form

> Author, with name reversed. "Minor Work Title in Quotation Marks." *Major Work Italicized.* Date of item if provided. URL: <in angle brackets>. Date you accessed it.

Titled Work Online, No Author Listed

Note Form

> [1]"Minor Work Title in Quotation Marks," *Major Work Italicized*, date of item if provided, URL: <in angle brackets>, date you accessed it.

Bibliographic Form

> "Minor Work Title in Quotation Marks." *Major Work Italicized.* Date of item if provided. URL: <in angle brackets>. Date you accessed it.

Keeping Up in the E-World

Citing sources for your work is always a challenge, made even more difficult by the wide variety of electronic sources. That difficulty can be eased, though, by following two basic guidelines: (1) Keep a citation reference book handy—this book, the *Chicago* manual, or Turabian; and (2) Use common sense in extrapolating formats from one type to another. Follow those two steps, and your chore will still be tedious, but you'll encounter less frustration in the citation process.

13

Handling Classified Material

Why?

Most students will neither have access to nor need to use classified material. This chapter applies only to intelligence professionals who regularly deal with classified material. Of course,
the guidance here is unclassified, and all regulations pertaining
to security clearance and need-to-know apply when handling
the material. Your organization's security officer should be able
to answer questions that arise.

If you use classified material for your paper, cite it in notes
and the bibliography just as you would any other source. Using
classified material will preclude publication of your paper or
thesis outside official channels. Security regulations prohibit
writers using information from official sources in unclassified
papers when the sources are not available to the general public.
An unclassified paper intended for public release, therefore,
must use and refer only to open, available sources. If any classified material is used, the paper must be appropriately classified.

These precautions, however, are not intended to discourage
your use of classified material. Certain government institutions
are unique in their intelligence professionals' ability to perform
in-depth research in classified sources. It is essential that proper
precautions be taken with this material.

Unclassified Excerpts from Classified Works

Because of the danger of compromise, *do not use unclassified excerpts from classified publications*. You must ensure that any such extract is handled appropriately. Even if the information you quote or paraphrase is unclassified, you must mark the paper with an appropriate distribution statement, and it cannot be handled outside official channels. See your security officer for the most current guidance.

How? Similarity to Unclassified Forms

Citing classified forms is so similar to citing unclassified forms that only a few examples are provided in this chapter. If you do not find a specific source here, refer to a similar unclassified source in *The Chicago Manual of Style* or Kate Turabian's *Manual for Writers of Research Papers, Theses, and Dissertations*, and extrapolate a form from there, adding the appropriate security markings.

Proper Precautions and Markings

Note: All examples in this chapter are unclassified. Classifications are notional, and are shown only to provide formats for student use.

Always keep security precautions in mind when you are dealing with classified material. Use proper markings and downgrading instructions on the cover sheet and title page. Mark the appropriate classification of each paragraph in the paper, even if it is unclassified (U).

When your paper is classified by "multiple sources," maintain a list of those sources. Your bibliography is an ideal place to list them. List classified sources in a separate section of your bibliography with the heading "Bibliography of Classified Sources." If you have any questions about the security aspects of your paper, see your security office.

Downgrading, Declassification, and Marking

General

Executive orders consistently emphasize the need to evaluate classified material periodically for possible downgrading or declassification. Department of Defense implementation of those executive orders requires that classified documents be marked with a statement showing how the material came to be classified ("Classified by . . .") and a declassification statement or, in many cases, a notice of exemption from downgrading ("Declassify on . . .").

This textbook is *not* a security manual, nor does it presume to offer detailed guidance on security matters. But it is important for intelligence analysts to understand proper procedures for marking classified material in a citation. Detailed guidance concerning these procedures can be found in security regulations available to your organization.

No Downgrading Shown?

If you must cite a classified document and it has no downgrading or declassification statement anywhere in the document, use the following statement at the end of the bibliographic entry (remember that these instructions are not required in the note form): Downgrading or declassification instructions not provided.

Note and Bibliographic Forms

Notes and bibliographies for classified material must reflect clearly your source for the information and must follow security regulations regarding the handling of classified material. One of the most important considerations in citing classified material is your identification of the product's security classification. Dissemination control markings such as "Orcon" (Dissemination and Extraction of Information Controlled by Originator) need not be spelled out. If you cite Orcon material, you must arrange officially for its release and include that release authorization with your paper.

If you have a source that does not correspond with any of the examples, use a commonsense approach. Use something analogous to the examples wherever possible, getting whatever guidance you can from your security officer. Just be sure to include enough information so that you or another reader with the appropriate clearance can find the item later.

A note or bibliographic entry for a classified source should contain the following items: classification of the entry, in parentheses; producer (author, if named, or originating organization); recipient, if appropriate (for example, for a letter, memorandum, message, or interview); title, with its classification; the classification of the document; date (for a message, use the date-time group); page number, if appropriate (for example, for a study or report); and remarks, if necessary. Include downgrading instructions as the last item *in the bibliographic entry only*; they are not necessary in the note form. A separate listing for the publisher and place of publication for classified products is not necessary, since that information is usually obvious.

Following are generic examples of note and bibliography forms for classified sources. The entries given as "Next Reference to the Same Source" under notes are examples of shortened subsequent references to the same source. In your bibliography, alphabetize by author if possible; otherwise, alphabetize by source—producing agency or command. Include all the information you used in the footnote or endnote, except page numbers of books. For articles, give their inclusive page numbers in the original publication. Do not number bibliographic entries.

The following generic example shows a bibliographic entry that reflects the positioning of each element, including classification markings. Use that example as a model for any classified source that you cite.

The example is a fictitious authored article from a classified "journal-type" publication, *Studies in Intelligence*, a journal that is also published in an unclassified version. If no author were listed, the entry would begin with the article title and would be alphabetized in the Bibliography of Classified Sources under the first word of the title, unless that word was *a*, *an*, or *the*. When they are used, retain military ranks or other titles in note and bibliographic forms. Include the branch of service where known.

Note: The examples shown here are unclassified. Classifications are notional, and are shown only to provide formats for student use.

Note Form

[1](U) Capt. John C. Marvel, USAF, "(U) The New Information War," SECRET//NOFORN//X1 article in S//NF//X1 *Studies in Intelligence* 52, no. 2 (2003): 5.

Next Reference to the Same Source

[2](U) Marvel, S//NF//X1 article, 7.

Bibliographic Form

(U) Marvel, John C., Capt., USAF. "(U) The New Information War." SECRET//NOFORN//X1 article in S//NF//X1 *Studies in Intelligence* 52, no. 2 (2003): 1-12. Classified by 2234568; declassify on X1.

Downgrading instructions are needed only in the bibliography. Note the placement of portion markings *before* each item they relate to.

Intelink

General

Intelink[1] provides remarkable access to Intelligence Community documents as well as many unclassified sources. Remember, though, that Intelink is available only to official users in secure areas, and citing sources from Intelink affects the handling of your paper. At a minimum, consider your paper "For Official Use Only" if you cite any source—classified or unclassified—from Intelink.

Security professionals have determined that the URL citation for an Intelink source is itself unclassified. So wherever possible, include that URL in your citation.

The following example is a notional article in a Defense Intelligence Agency product that is often cited in student papers. Adapt this format to other sources you take from Intelink, combining where necessary with related unclassified forms from chapters 11 and 12. Note, too, that many sources accessed on Intelink will not have page numbers. In that case, simply omit that portion of the note entry. Again, the classifications in the citations are notional.

Note Form

[1](C//NF) Defense Intelligence Agency, "(C//NF) Panaragua: Will Its Forces Participate in Peacekeeping?" C//NF article in S//NF *Military Intelligence Digest* 053-03, 22 March 2003, URL: <http://delphi.dia.ic.gov/intel/world_wide/disp/mid/2003>, accessed on Intelink 5 April 2003. Cited hereafter as DIA, "Panaragua."

Next Reference to the Same Source

[2](U) DIA, "Panaragua."

Bibliographic Form

This entry is classified (notionally) because the *title* is classified.

(C//NF) Defense Intelligence Agency. "(C//NF) Panaragua: Will Its Forces Participate in Peacekeeping?" C//NF article in S//NF *Military Intelligence Digest* 053-03, 22 March 2003. URL: <http://delphi .dia.ic.gov/intel/world_wide/ disp/mid/2003>. Accessed on Intelink 5 April 2003. Derived from Multiple Sources; declassify on X1.

Even if the document you retrieve from Intelink is unclassified, it is not a good security practice to cite Intelink-derived materials in unclassified papers, especially if you hope to release the material outside U.S. Government channels.

Note for Chapter 13

1. For an unclassified account of how Intelink came to be, see Fredrick Thomas Martin, *Top Secret Intranet: How U.S. Intelligence Built Intelink—The World's Largest, Most Secure Network* (Upper Saddle River, NJ: Prentice Hall, 1998).

Bibliography

Adelstein, Michael E., and Jean G. Pival. *The Writing Commitment*, 5th ed. Fort Worth: Harcourt Brace Jovanovich, 1993.

Barry, Dave. *Classic Dave Barry Calendar*. Kansas City, MO: Andrews McMeel Publishing, April 5/6, 2008.

Berg, Bruce. *Qualitative Research Methods for the Social Sciences*, 3d ed. Boston: Allyn and Bacon, 1998.

Cavender, Nancy, and Howard Kahane. *Argument and Persuasion: Text and Readings for Writers*. Belmont, CA: Wadsworth Publishing, 1989.

Central Intelligence Agency, Directorate of Intelligence. *Style Manual and Writers Guide for Intelligence Publications*, 5th ed. Langley, VA: CIA, October 1996.

The Chicago Manual of Style, 15th ed. Chicago: The University of Chicago Press, 2003.

Colligan, William E., Captain, USA. *The Privatization of Personnel Security: The Effects of the National Performance Review on the Intelligence Community*. MSSI Thesis. Washington, DC: Joint Military Intelligence College, August 1996.

Don, Peter J., Captain, U.S. Army. *The Awakening: Developing Military Intelligence Professionals to Support United States Army Special Forces*. MSSI Thesis. Washington, DC: Joint Military Intelligence College, 1998.

Ford, Ronnie, Captain, USA. *Tet 1968: Understanding the Surprise*. MSSI Thesis. Washington, DC: Joint Military Intelligence College, July1993.

———. *Tet 1968: Understanding the Surprise*. London: Frank Cass, 1995.

Fulkerson, Richard. *Teaching the Argument in Writing*. Urbana, IL: National Council of Teachers of English, 1996.

Garner, Diane L., and Diane H. Smith. *The Complete Guide to Citing Government Documents: A Manual for Writers and Librarians*. Rev. ed. Bethesda, MD: Congressional Information Service, 1993.

Gertz, Bill. "Bush Pressures Putin to Stop Arms Sales." *Washington Times*, 25 March 2003, A1.

Hale, Constance, and Jessie Scanlon. *Wired Style: Principles of English Usage in the Digital Age*. Rev. updated ed. New York: Broadway Books, 1999.

Hodges, John C., and Mary E. Whitten. *Harbrace College Handbook*, 12th rev. ed. New York: Harcourt Brace Jovanovich, 1995.

Hoover, Kenneth, and Todd Donovan. *The Elements of Social Scientific Thinking*, 6th ed. New York: St. Martin's Press, 1995.

Horner, Winifred Bryan. *Rhetoric in the Classical Tradition*. New York: St. Martin's Press, 1988.

Huntington, Samuel P. "Coping with the Lippman Gap." *Foreign Affairs* 66, no. 3 (1988).

Johnson, J. B., and Richard Joslyn. *Political Science Research Methods*, 3d ed. Washington, DC: Congressional Quarterly, 1995.

Johnson, James William. *Logic and Rhetoric*. New York: Macmillan, 1962.

Joint Forces Staff College, National Defense University. *Joint Forces Staff College Style Manual*. JFSC Pub 4. Norfolk, VA: JFSC, January 2004.

Kroll, Barry M. "How College Freshmen View Plagiarism." *Written Communication* 5 (1988): 203–21.

Kuhn, Thomas. *The Structure of Scientific Revolutions*, 2d ed., enlarged. Chicago: University of Chicago Press, 1970.

Leedy, Paul, and Jeanne Ellis Ormrod. *Practical Research: Planning and Design*, 7th ed. Upper Saddle River, NJ: Merrill Prentice-Hall, 2001.

Levin, Gerald. *The Macmillan College Handbook*, 2d ed. New York: Macmillan, 1991.

Magnan, Stephen W., Captain, U.S. Air Force. *Information Operations: Are We Our Own Worst Enemy?* MSSI Thesis. Washington, DC: Joint Military Intelligence College, 1998.

Major, James S. *Communicating with Intelligence: Writing and Briefing in the Intelligence and National Security Communities*. Lanham, MD: Scarecrow Press, 2008.

———. *Style: Usage, Composition, and Form*. Washington, DC: Defense Intelligence Agency, 2000.

———. *Writing with Intelligence*. Washington, DC: Defense Intelligence Agency, 1995.

Martin, Fredrick Thomas. *Top Secret Intranet: How U.S. Intelligence Built Intelink—The World's Largest, Most Secure Network.* Upper Saddle River, NJ: Prentice Hall, 1998.

Maxwell, Joseph A. *Qualitative Research Design.* Vol. 41 of the Applied Social Research Methods Series. Thousand Oaks, CA: Sage Publications, 1996.

Mayberry, Katherine J., and Robert E. Golden. *For Argument's Sake: A Guide to Writing Effective Arguments*, 2d ed. New York: Harper Collins, 1996.

Merriam-Webster's Collegiate Dictionary. 10th ed. Springfield, MA: Merriam-Webster, 1993.

Meyer, Herbert E., and Jill M. Meyer. *How to Write.* Washington, DC: Storm King Press, 1986.

Ogden, Evelyn Hunt. *Completing Your Doctoral Dissertation or Master's Thesis in Two Semesters or Less*, 2d ed. Lancaster, PA: Technomic, 1993.

Petersen, Martin. "Managing/Teaching New Analysts." *Studies in Intelligence*, unclassified edition (Fall 1986).

Random House Dictionary of the English Language, 2d ed., 2000.

Schoomaker, Peter J., General, USA. "Special Operations." *Army* (April 1998).

Seyler, Dorothy M. *Understanding Argument: A Text with Readings.* New York: McGraw Hill, 1994.

Shaw, Harry. *Punctuate It Right!* New York: Harper & Row, 1963.

Strunk, William Jr., and E. B. White. *The Elements of Style.* 4th ed. Boston: Allyn and Bacon, 2000.

Turabian, Kate L. *A Manual for Writers of Term Papers, Theses, and Dissertations*, 7th ed. Chicago: The University of Chicago Press, 2007.

United States Government Printing Office Style Manual. Washington, DC: GPO, 2000.

White, Louise. *Political Analysis: Techniques and Practice*, 3d ed. New York: Harcourt Brace, 1994.

Yin, Robert K. *Case Study Research: Design and Methods*, 2d ed. Vol. 5 of the Applied Social Research Methods Series. Thousand Oaks, CA: Sage Publications, 1994.

Index

About the Author

James S. ("Jim") Major spent more than 40 years in intelligence, serving in both military and civilian capacities, in assignments at the tactical, operational, strategic, and national levels.

Major was commissioned from Army ROTC in 1963. After Airborne and Ranger training at Fort Benning, Georgia, he served as an infantry officer in West Germany. In 1966 he transferred to the Military Intelligence (MI) branch and went to Fort Holabird, Maryland, for basic MI training. Following a 1-year advisory tour in Pleiku, Vietnam, he returned to Fort Holabird for advanced intelligence training. There he entered Foreign Area Officer training for Indonesia and spent a year in Bandung, West Java, at the Indonesian Army Command and General Staff College. Returning to Ohio University, he earned a master's degree in international affairs, specializing in Indonesia and Southwest Asia. He then served three years with the Defense Intelligence Agency (DIA) at Arlington Hall Station, Virginia.

In 1975, "Major Major" moved to Fort Gordon, Georgia, where he established and commanded the first Special Security Detachment at the U.S. Army Signal School. Promoted to Lieutenant Colonel in 1978, he served in Germany as a Plans Officer and later a Division Chief on the V (U.S.) Corps staff. In 1980 he was reassigned to Defense Intelligence Agency (DIA) at the Pentagon, where he was first the Intelligence Support Coordinator for NATO, then the Executive Officer to Mr. John T. Hughes, the senior civilian in DIA. In 1982 he transferred to Tampa, Florida, where he served as DIA's first Liaison Officer to the U.S. Central Command and the U.S. Readiness Command. He returned to Washington in September 1985 and joined the faculty of the Joint Military Intelligence College (JMIC). He retired from the Army in November 1988, and as a government civilian, created the Writing Center at the JMIC.

Major wrote 15 books that were published by the U.S. Government. Those include the textbooks *Writing with Intelligence*, *Briefing with Intelligence*, and *Wordshops*, as well as the JMIC style manual (*Style: Usage, Composition, and Form*), and two editions of a book on footnotes and bibliographies entitled *Citation*. In 2008, Scarecrow Press published his book *Communicating with Intelligence: Writing and Briefing in the Intelligence and National Security Communities*, the first book in the Scarecrow Press Intelligence Education Series.

Major has also published articles and anecdotes in regional and national publications, including *The Washington Times*, *Quarterly Review of Doublespeak*, *The Writing Lab Newsletter*, *Spell-Binder*, and *Army* magazine. In 1994 he received the JMIC award for Excellence in Teaching, presented to the Outstanding Faculty Member of the Year. In 1997, he was awarded the National Intelligence Medal of Achievement.

Major's military awards include the Legion of Merit, Defense Meritorious Service Medal with two Oak Leaf Clusters, Bronze Star Medal, Cross of Gallantry with Palm, Presidential Unit Citation, Airborne Wings, and Ranger Tab. Jim and his wife, Joan, live in Arlington, Virginia, with their miniature Australian shepherds, Amber and Glory.